T0288597

Benchmarks for Success

Expected Short- and Long-Term Outcomes of
National Guard Youth ChalleNGe Participants

KATHRYN A. EDWARDS

Prepared for the Office of the Secretary of Defense
Approved for public release; distribution unlimited

NATIONAL DEFENSE RESEARCH INSTITUTE

For more information on this publication, visit www.rand.org/t/RRA271-1

Library of Congress Cataloging-in-Publication Data is available for this publication.
ISBN: 978-1-9774-0497-8

Published by the RAND Corporation, Santa Monica, Calif.
© Copyright 2020 RAND Corporation
RAND® is a registered trademark.

Support RAND
Make a tax-deductible charitable contribution at
www.rand.org/giving/contribute

www.rand.org

Preface

The National Guard Youth ChalleNGe program is a residential, quasi-military program for youths ages 16 to 18 who are experiencing difficulty in traditional high school. Participating states, through their state National Guard organizations with supporting federal funds and oversight, operate the program. The program includes a 5.5-month Residential Phase followed by a 12-month Post-Residential Phase. Each participant is supported by a mentor throughout both phases. The stated goal of Youth ChalleNGe is "to intervene in and reclaim the lives of 16–18-year-old high school dropouts, producing program graduates with the values, life skills, education, and self-discipline necessary to succeed as productive citizens" (National Guard Youth ChalleNGe, undated).

The Office of the Assistant Secretary of Defense for Manpower and Reserve Affairs asked the RAND Corporation to develop a set of measures that focus on various aspects of Youth ChalleNGe with an overall goal of improving program effectiveness. The RAND team's analyses of Youth ChalleNGe began in September 2016; ongoing efforts were expected to continue through June 2020. This report focuses on postprogram measures of success. The objective is to provide program staff with benchmarked expectations of short- and long-term outcomes of participants in their program, based on the outcomes of similar individuals in large, nationally representative surveys.

This report will be of greatest interest to Youth ChalleNGe program staff and directors at individual sites. It will also be of interest to personnel providing oversight for the Youth ChalleNGe program, staff at similarly targeted youth intervention programs, and policymakers concerned with designing effective youth programs or determining appropriate metrics by which to track progress in youth programs.

This research was sponsored by the Office of the Assistant Secretary of Defense for Manpower and Reserve Affairs and conducted within the Forces and Resources Policy Center of the RAND National Security Research Division (NSRD), which operates the National Defense Research Institute (NDRI), a federally funded research and development center sponsored by the Office of the Secretary of Defense, the Joint Staff, the Unified Combatant Commands, the Navy, the Marine Corps, the defense agencies, and the defense intelligence enterprise.

For more information on the RAND Forces and Resources Policy Center, see www.rand.org/nsrd/frp or contact the director (contact information is provided on the webpage).

Contents

Preface iii

Box and Figure vii

Tables ix

Summary xi

Acknowledgments xxiii

Abbreviations xxv

CHAPTER ONE

High School Dropouts and Intervention Programs 1

Objective of This Report 3

Prior Research on High School Dropouts 4

Methodological Approach of This Report 15

Organization of This Report 18

CHAPTER TWO

Data Sources 19

The Current Population Survey, October Supplements, 1996–2016 19

National Longitudinal Survey of Youth, 1997 Cohort 22

The Education Longitudinal Study of 2002 24

Comparisons Across the Samples 25

CHAPTER THREE

Benchmarks During the Dropout Period 27

Demographics 27

Family 33

Academic 40

Conclusions 44

CHAPTER FOUR
Benchmarks of Short- and Long-Term Outcomes 47
Status the Year After Leaving School 47
Credentials and Training 49
Employment and Earnings 52
Civics 58
Health and Well-Being 62
Conclusions 64

CHAPTER FIVE
Benchmarks of Success 67
Preprogram Benchmarks: Background Characteristics, Ages 14 to 16 67
Postprogram Benchmarks: Immediate Outcomes, Ages 17 to 19 72
Postprogram Benchmarks: Longer-Term Outcomes, Ages 20 to 29 75
Conclusion 80

References 81

Box and Figure

Box

1.1.   Glossary of Terms... 5

Figure

4.1.   Share of High School Dropouts Earning a GED,
         by Age GED Awarded (NLSY, 1997 Cohort).................... 51

Tables

S.1. Range of Characteristics of Benchmark Groups,
      Ages 14–16 xv
S.2. Range of Characteristics of Benchmark Groups,
      Ages 17–19... xviii
S.3. Range of Outcomes of Benchmark Groups, Ages 20–29...... xxi
1.1. Features of Three Federally Funded Youth Intervention
      Programs.. 14
2.1. Summary of Data Sources and Sample Comparison
      Concerns... 26
3.1. Demographic Means of Dropouts in the Year After
      Leaving School, by Final Grade Attended (CPS) 28
3.2. Demographic Means of Dropouts, GED Holders, and
      High School Graduates Who Do Not Enroll in College at
      Age 16 (NLSY) and Grade 10 (ELS)........................... 30
3.3. Comparison of CPS, NLSY, and ELS Dropouts with
      Samples of Previous Studies of Youth
      Intervention Programs 32
3.4. Means of Family Characteristics of Dropouts in the Year
      After Leaving School, by Final Grade Attended (CPS) 34
3.5. Means of Family Characteristics of Dropouts, GED
      Holders, and High School Graduates Who Do Not Enroll
      in College at Age 16 (NLSY) and Grade 10 (ELS)............. 36
3.6. Means of Individual Characteristics of Dropouts, GED
      Holders, and High School Graduates Who Do Not Enroll
      in College at Age 16 (NLSY).....................................39
3.7. Means of Academic Characteristics of Dropouts, GED
      Holders, and High School Graduates Who Do Not Enroll
      in College at Age 16 (NLSY) and Grade 10 (ELS)............. 40

4.1.   Means of Near-Term Outcomes of Dropouts in the Year
        After Leaving School, by Final Grade Attended (CPS) 48
4.2.   Share of Dropouts with a GED, by Age (NLSY) 50
4.3.   Share of GED Holders Who Are Enrolled in Two-Year or
        Four-Year Colleges, by Age (NLSY) 51
4.4.   Vocational Enrollment Rates Among Benchmark Groups,
        by Age (CPS) 52
4.5.   Labor Force Nonparticipation Rates Among Benchmark
        Groups, by Age (CPS) 53
4.6.   Share of Benchmark Groups Who Did Not Have a Job in
        the Prior Year, by Age (NLSY) 54
4.7.   Share of Individuals Employed and Job Characteristics of
        Employed Workers in Benchmark Groups, by Age (CPS) 55
4.8.   Earnings of Employed Workers in Benchmark Groups,
        by Age (CPS) 57
4.9.   Annual Earned Income Among Benchmark Groups, in
        Thousands, by Age (NLSY) 58
4.10. Self-Reported Arrest Rates Across Benchmark Groups,
        by Age (NLSY) 59
4.11. Voter Participation Rates Among Benchmark Groups,
        Minimum and Maximum, by Age (ELS) 60
4.12. Voter Participation Rates Among Benchmark Groups,
        Minimum and Maximum, by Election (NLSY) 61
4.13. Volunteer Rates Among Benchmark Groups, by Age (ELS) ... 61
4.14. Volunteer Rates Among Benchmark Groups, by Year
        and Age (NLSY) 61
4.15. Military Service Rates Among Benchmark Groups, by Age
        (ELS) 62
4.16. Rates of Underweight and Obesity Across Benchmark
        Groups, by Age (NLSY) 63
4.17. Share of Benchmark Groups Who Live with Their Parents,
        by Age (CPS) 64
4.18. Rates of Marriage and Divorce Across Benchmark Groups,
        by Age (NLSY) 65
5.1.   Range of Characteristics of Benchmark Groups,
        Ages 14 to 16 72
5.2.   Range of Characteristics of Benchmark Groups,
        Ages 17 to 19 75
5.3.   Range of Outcomes of Benchmark Groups, Ages 20 to 29 ... 80

Summary

Background

The National Guard Youth ChalleNGe program (hereafter referred to as ChalleNGe) is a residential, quasi-military program for youths ages 16 to 18 who are experiencing academic difficulties and exhibiting problem behaviors, either inside or outside school; have dropped out or are in jeopardy of dropping out; and, in some cases, have had run-ins with the law. The ChalleNGe program runs for a total of 17.5 months, broken into a 5.5-month Residential Phase (a two-week acclimation period called Pre-ChalleNGe and five-month ChalleNGe) followed by a 12-month Post-Residential Phase. More than 220,000 young people have taken part in the ChalleNGe program, and nearly 165,000 have completed the program.

ChalleNGe is a national program that spans 39 sites in 28 states, the District of Columbia, and Puerto Rico. Participating states operate the program with supporting federal funds and oversight from state National Guard organizations. Each individual site is run by a site director. In this report, we refer to the national ChalleNGe program as the *program* or the *intervention*, whereas we refer to the site-specific programs as *sites*. Sites can develop their own, site-specific policy.

In 2005–2008 the ChalleNGe program was evaluated in a randomized controlled trial (RCT), the gold-standard method of program evaluation. The RCT's results concluded that the ChalleNGe intervention was successful; invitation to the program was associated with increased educational attainment and earnings through the three years following the end of the program. Using these differences, it has been estimated that ChalleNGe is a cost-effective program (see Bloom, Gardenhire-Crooks, and Mandsager, 2009; Millenky, Bloom, and Dillon, 2010; Millenky et al., 2011; Perez-Arce et al., 2012).

Yet, the successful RCT evaluation of the ChalleNGe program—and the validation of the ChalleNGe model—still leaves questions for individual sites about their own success. There are many ways in which a site's cadets may differ from the average cadet, or the average cadet from the RCT participants over a decade ago. Moreover, within ChalleNGe, there is considerable variation across sites in institutional settings, constraints, and goals (see Wenger et al., 2019, for the most recent review of sites). Given that the RCT included special follow-up surveys designed specifically for the evaluation, sites cannot generate comparable statistics to compare their graduates to the RCT's findings. An RCT, in short, does not necessarily provide sites or program staff a usable reference for what success means.

At the same time, all ChalleNGe sites collect data on their incoming cadets and follow their graduates for a 12-month period. Although sites can and do look for trends in their own site over time through these data, they do not have a way to gauge their progress toward a set of expected outcomes.

Objective of This Report

The objective of this report is to provide ChalleNGe sites with a set of population benchmarks to which to compare their cadets. We developed these benchmarks using data from large, household surveys and examining individuals who were similar to cadets. Rather than establish a control group and follow members over time, as is done in an RCT, we instead devised a set of population averages that site directors can use as a reasonable comparison to their Youth ChalleNGe participants at any time. In this way, our benchmarks can help site directors and staff on the ground gauge their own site's performance.

Our benchmarks fell into two groups, based on time period: around the time of dropping out and in the years following. These comparisons can be thought of as a snapshot at enrollment in ChalleNGe (the preprogram period) and a snapshot after ChalleNGe is completed (the postprogram period), respectively. The preperiod discussion was meant to inform site directors of how their incoming participant population differs from the population benchmarks and, in doing so, help site directors identify unique challenges or obstacles present among participants at their site. The postperiod discussion was meant to help directors interpret the 12-month follow-ups of cadets that they collect and help cadets with their post-residential plans. Both comparisons may help inform expectations of how participants will fare after the program.

Analytic Approach

We established a set of population benchmarks to inform site directors in developing expectations of reasonable outcomes for their program participants. The goal of these benchmarks was to provide a framework for interpreting long-term cadet outcomes that distinguishes between expected outcomes and successful outcomes and, in the process, identifies unrealistic outcomes.

Our means of doing this was to create comparison groups for ChalleNGe participants. As we noted previously, a key obstacle in evaluating a program is selection into program participation. An RCT solves this by pooling successful applicants and randomizing their participation. We solved this by analyzing three populations that represented the scope of potential selection for ChalleNGe:

- high school dropouts who did not get an equivalent credential (we referred to these as *dropouts*)
- high school dropouts who did get an equivalent credential (we referred to these as General Educational Development *[GED] holders*)
- high school graduates who did not attend college (we referred to these as *graduates*).

These groups should not be thought of as *good* and *bad* populations or as *starting* and *goal* populations; they were meant to represent the potential set of ChalleNGe participants and spanned what we referred to as the *spectrum of selection*.

We identified these three groups—which we refer to as the *benchmark groups*—in three large public surveys: the Current Population Survey (CPS), the National Longitudinal Survey of Youth (NLSY), and the Education Longitudinal Study (ELS). We found the population average for each benchmark group for an array of outcome measures. These averages were the benchmarks that we presented for site directors.

Preprogram Benchmarks: Background Characteristics, Ages 14–16

The literature regarding high school dropouts identified characteristics that correlate with not getting a high school diploma: demographic correlates, socioeconomic correlates (which we divided into family and individual characteristics), and academic correlates. When we compared the benchmark groups at ages 14 to 16 in the CPS, NLSY, and ELS, we found the following:

- All three benchmark groups were disproportionately more male and less white than high school graduates who go to college.
- Dropouts and GED holders were similar on family background correlates.
- GED holders were more likely to report engaging in risky behavior outside of school than either dropouts or graduates but had similar behavior to dropouts inside school.
- GED holders were much more similar in aptitude and test scores to graduates than to dropouts.

We distilled these findings and other measures into Table S.1, which provides the range of the benchmark groups along key measures. This table was intended to serve as a reference for ChalleNGe

Table S.1
Range of Characteristics of Benchmark Groups, Ages 14–16

Characteristic	Range	Source
Demographic and Family		
Male	55–61%	CPS, NLSY, ELS
White (non-Hispanic)	39–68%	CPS, NLSY, ELS
Black (non-Hispanic)	15–24%	CPS, NLSY, ELS
Hispanic[a]	14–29%	CPS, NLSY, ELS
Two–biological parent family	25–51%	NLSY, ELS
Single-parent family	24–41%	NLSY, ELS
Mother was high school dropout	17–45%	NLSY, ELS
Father was high school dropout	18–44%	NLSY, ELS
Deceased primary family member[b]	4–5%	NLSY
Family/home risk score[c]	3.2–4.1	NLSY
Physical environment risk score[c]	1.5–2	NLSY
Gun violence witness	12–20%	NLSY
Individual		
Reported previous sexual activity	30–52%	NLSY
Reported drinking alcohol	51–61%	NLSY
Reported smoking marijuana	27–42%	NLSY
Emotional disorder[d]	3–7%	NLSY
Learning disorder	6–9%	NLSY
Underweight	8–11%	NLSY
Overweight	16–20%	NLSY
Obese	9–11%	NLSY
Academic		
Armed Services Vocational Aptitude Battery percentile (1 = low)[e]	22–34	NLSY
Repeated a grade	18–50%	NLSY, ELS

Table S.1—Continued

Characteristic	Range	Source
Lowest quartile of math and reading[f]	25–48%	ELS
Has an individualized education program[g]	13–32%	ELS
In-school dropout prevention program	4–7%	ELS
Remedial math or English class	13–14%	ELS
In-school suspension	16–38%	ELS
Out-of-school suspension	11–25%	ELS

NOTES: This table presents, for each variable listed, the range of sample averages of dropouts, GED holders, and graduates in the survey listed in the rightmost column. Listing of multiple surveys indicates that the variable was found in multiple surveys, and the range spans the sample averages of all three surveys. For the CPS, data are from the 1996–2016 October supplements of the CPS; supplement weights were used. Dropouts in the CPS are identified by indicating in the initial October survey having been enrolled and, in the second survey, 12 months later, that they were not enrolled and had not received a diploma. For the NLSY, members of the 1997 NLSY sample reached age 16 in the 1997–2001 waves, depending on age at sample start. The sample is weighted using the panel weights. For the ELS, the ELS 2002 is a sample of tenth-graders; means are weighted with base-year student weight.

[a] Hispanic and white (or black) are not exclusive categories, in that white or black is race and Hispanic is ethnicity. We define *Hispanic* as an ethnic group and remove from the black and white race categories anyone of Hispanic ethnicity, to make the categories mutually exclusive.

[b] *Deceased primary family member* indicates that a parent or sibling has died.

[c] Family/home risk score is based on Caldwell and Bradley (1984) and ranges from 0 to 21. Physical environment risk score is a subset of Family/home and ranges from 0 to 7. For each, a higher index indicates higher risk.

[d] *Emotional disorder* encompasses eating disorders; more information can be found in Appendix 9 of the NLSY codebook (National Longitudinal Surveys, undated).

[e] Armed Services Vocational Aptitude Battery percentile is based on three-month age groups, discussed in Appendix 10 of the NLSY codebook supplement (National Longitudinal Surveys, undated). Benchmark groups are statistically different from overall NLSY sample.

[f] The ELS survey instrument includes math and reading tests (see section 2.2.2 of the ELS User Manual National Center for Education Statistics, undated; the quartile score divides the weighted achievement distribution into four equal groups.

[g] An individualized education program (IEP) is required by federal law for any student with a disability.

site directors to gauge how their sites' participants may differ from the average among the target population. The range covered the high and low mean values of the benchmark groups—often, though not always, set by dropouts and graduates.

Postprogram Benchmarks: Immediate Outcomes, Ages 17–19

The age range for the ChalleNGe program is 16 to 18, aligning ChalleNGe's intervention with the time in or immediately after leaving school. We compared outcomes of the benchmark groups over ages 17 to 19 in the CPS, NLSY, and ELS. These were our findings:

- More than half of dropouts obtained a GED by their late 20s, but the most common ages of attainment are 17 to 20 years old.
- Enrollment in vocational school was low among dropouts and GED holders.
- A large share of recent dropouts was out of the labor force, neither working nor looking for work.

We distilled these findings and others into Table S.2. This table was intended to serve as a reference for site directors to compare their own site's placement statistics with target population averages at similar ages. In the first column, we showed the baseline outcomes of dropouts and GED holders ages 17 and 18. In the second, we showed the range of the benchmark groups at age 19. The reason for this is that graduates are still enrolled full time in high school through age 18, and the comparison would not be appropriate at that age.

The way to interpret Table S.2, then, is this: The left column examining 17- and 18-year-old dropouts was the baseline expectation of how cadets fare after the program, rates on which ChalleNGe hopes to improve. The right column examining the benchmark groups at age 19 established reasonable limits to those improvements. Thus, site directors should not expect that a 16-year-old cadet who finishes the Residential Phase will have better outcomes at 17 and 18 than a high school graduate with a diploma has at 19.

Table S.2
Range of Characteristics of Benchmark Groups, Ages 17–19

Characteristic	Dropouts and GED Holders Only, 17–18 Years Old	All Benchmark Groups, 19 Years Old	Source
GED attainment	10–18%	28%[a]	NLSY
Enrolled in vocational school	3–4%	2–4%	CPS
Employed	30–43%	45–65%	CPS
Full time[b]	38–43%	56–63%	CPS
Paid hourly	88–94%	88–93%	CPS
In the service sector[c,d]		44%	CPS
In food service[c,d]		16–20%	CPS
Hourly wage[c]		$10.67–11.12	CPS
Not in the labor force	41–55%	19–36%	CPS
Lives with parents[c]		64–80%	CPS
Self-reported arrest[e]		6–15%	NLSY
Underweight[f]		4–7%	NLSY

NOTE: This table presents, for each variable listed, the range of sample averages of dropouts, GED holders, and graduates in the survey listed in the third column. Listing of multiple surveys indicates that the variable was found in multiple surveys, and the range spans the sample averages of all three surveys. For the NLSY, data are from the 1997–2015 waves of the NLSY. The sample is weighted using the panel weights. For the CPS, data are from the 1996–2016 October supplements of the CPS; supplement weights were used. Dropouts in the CPS are identified by indicating in the initial October survey their being enrolled and, in the second survey, 12 months later, that they were not enrolled and had not received a diploma. We assume 17- and 18-year-olds correspond to tenth- and eleventh-grade school leavers. Hourly wages are adjusted to real 2016 dollars.
[a] This estimate refers to dropouts only and captures GED attainment by age 19.
[b] A full-time worker is one who usually works 35 hours or more each week at their main job.
[c] We do not show estimates for 17- and 18-year-olds for certain categories owing to data or definitional concerns.
[d] The service sector consists of CPS-defined categories of occupations: food preparation and service; building and grounds cleaning and maintenance; personal care and service; and sales and related. *Food service* refers to food preparation and service only.
[e] Self-reported arrest covers a one-year period, defined as the 12 months prior to the most recent interview.
[f] Individuals are classified as underweight or obese using the body mass index measure included in the survey.

Postprogram Benchmarks: Longer-Term Outcomes, Ages 20–29

ChalleNGe graduates are tracked for only 12 months after finishing the program; sites do not keep count of longer-term outcomes, which we defined as those occurring before age 29. However, the literature regarding high school dropouts indicates that not having a high school diploma is associated with worse performance in the labor market, measured either through earnings or employment; worse physical and mental health; higher rates of arrest, substance abuse, and smoking; and higher likelihood of being on government assistance. These were our key findings in comparing the benchmark groups over this period in the CPS, NLSY, and ELS:

- A small but significant share of the benchmark groups attained an occupational or technical certificate.
- Enrollment in two-year or four-year postsecondary education was low (less than 5 percent) for GED holders.
- Labor force participation varied greatly across the benchmark groups.
- The difference in annual income between the groups started small but grew with age, likely because of labor force participation.
- In terms of negative civic outcomes, self-reported arrest rates were highest among dropouts but were not zero among graduates. For all groups, arrests fell with age.
- In terms of positive civic outcomes, self-reported volunteering and voting rates varied with education; dropouts voted and volunteered the least, and graduates voted and volunteered the most. For all groups, voting and volunteering increased with age.
- Military service was similar for graduates and GED holders.
- Among measures of well-being, there were few differences between the benchmark groups: They had similar rates of obesity, underweight, marriage, divorce, and independent living.

In Table S.3, we showed the range of the benchmark groups along key measures. We divided our table into two age ranges: In the left columns, we looked at the range of averages between ages 20 and 24, and, in the right column, we looked at the range of averages between ages 25 and 29. Given that site directors did not have data for their former cadets in this age range, these estimates were meant to help directors understand their participants' needs and challenges *after* the program ends and possibly influence a site's policy to take those challenges or needs into account.

Conclusion

The Youth ChalleNGe program is an intensive intervention into the lives of 16- to 18-year-old youths who have dropped out of high school. Programs draw participants from a portion of the population who often come from risky or difficult backgrounds and who are expected to have worse outcomes into the long term. Although there is a clear and reliable method for evaluating the program design through an RCT, the RCT results are often not interpretable or cost-effectively replicable for an individual site within a program.

Using public survey data from various sources, we produced detailed descriptive estimates of three groups: high school dropouts, GED holders, and high school graduates who did not attend college. We compared these groups at different ages to provide an informative, numeric reference of the target population from ages 14 to 29. This report was intended to be used by directors to put numbers to backgrounds and outcomes to support their sites' program and policy development. Our aim was not only to help sites identify unique needs but also to give sites references with which to measure their own success.

Table S.3
Range of Outcomes of Benchmark Groups, Ages 20–29

Outcome	20–24 Years Old	25–29 Years Old	Source
Credentials and training			
Dropouts with GED[a]	34–51%	52–62%	NLSY
GED holders enrolled in college[b]	4–6%	3–9%	NLSY
Enrolled in vocational school	1–4%		CPS
Has occupational/technical certificate		14–18%	ELS
Employment and earnings			
Employed	49–73%		CPS
Full time[c]	61–79%		CPS
Paid hourly	82–93%		CPS
In service sector[d]	31–45%		CPS
In food service[d]	9–17%		CPS
Hourly wage[e]	$10.20–13.61		CPS
Not in the labor force	20–37%		CPS
Did not work during the prior year[e]	13–37%	15–39%	NLSY
Annual earnings (thousands)[f]	$7.1–20.6	$14.20–30.20	NLSY
Civics			
Self-reported arrest[g]	4–12%	2–8%	NLSY
Voted	14–39%	17–45%	ELS, NLSY
Volunteered	15–30%	18–39%	ELS, NLSY
In military service	1–4%	0–4%	ELS
Health and well-being			
Underweight[h]	2–5%	2–5%	NLSY
Obese[h]	19–28%	29–41%	NLSY
Lives with parents	28–70%		CPS

Table S.3—Continued

Outcome	20–24 Years Old	25–29 Years Old	Source
Married	14–30%	24–42%	NLSY
Divorced	1–10%	7–14%	NLSY

NOTES: This table presents, for each variable listed, the range of sample averages of dropouts, GED holders, and graduates in the survey listed in the third column. Listing multiple surveys indicates that the variable was found in multiple surveys, and the range spans the sample averages of all three surveys. For the NLSY, data are from the 1997–2015 waves of the NLSY. The sample is weighted using the panel weights. For the CPS, data are from the 1996–2016 October supplements of the CPS; supplement weights were used. Dropouts in the CPS are identified by indicating in the initial October survey their being enrolled and, in the second survey, 12 months later, that they were not enrolled and had not received a diploma. For the ELS, data are from the age 21 and age 27 waves of the ELS; adjusted using follow-up weights from wave 2–3.

[a] This is the share of all dropouts who have a GED. The range indicates the range over the ages listed, not the surveys used.

[b] Covers two- and four-year colleges but describes exclusively GED holders.

[c] Full-time workers are those who usually work 35 hours or more each week at their main job.

[d] The service sector comprises CPS-defined categories of occupations: food preparation and service; building and grounds cleaning and maintenance; personal care and service; sales and related. *Food service* is food preparation and service only.

[e] Consists of individuals who did not work and earned $0.

[f] Hourly wages and annual income are adjusted to real 2016 dollars.

[g] Self-reported arrest covers a one-year period, defined as the 12 months prior to the most recent interview.

[h] Individuals are classified as underweight or obese using the body mass index measure included in the survey.

Acknowledgments

We are grateful to the staff of the National Guard Youth ChalleNGe program. We thank the many staff who granted the author interviews that provided detailed information and thoughtful insight as to program needs during the course of site visits. Their opinions greatly aided the motivation and design of this report.

We are also grateful to our RAND colleagues for their support: Jennie Wenger, Stephani Wrabel, and Louay Constant provided reviews and comments on portions of the report. Craig Bond reviewed the report; Kristin Leuschner edited the report and made many improvements for clarity and ease of reading. We thank all who contributed to this research or assisted with this report, but we retain full responsibility for the accuracy, objectivity, and analytical integrity of the work presented here.

Abbreviations

ASVAB   Armed Services Vocational Aptitude Battery

BMI   body mass index

CPS   Current Population Survey

ELS   Education Longitudinal Study

GED   General Educational Development

IEP   individualized education program

NCES   National Center for Education Statistics

NLSY   National Longitudinal Survey of Youth

RCT   randomized controlled trial

CHAPTER ONE

High School Dropouts and Intervention Programs

According to the most recent data compiled by the National Center for Education Statistics (NCES), about 7 percent of 16- to 24-year-olds in the United States neither are enrolled in high school nor have received a high school diploma or alternative credential such as the General Educational Development (GED); 18 percent of high school freshmen fail to graduate from high school within four years (McFarland, Cui, and Stark, 2018).[1] Decades of research show that dropping out of high school is the result of a long process, one that often starts years before departing school. Not having a diploma is correlated with poor outcomes over the lifetime: High school dropouts are more likely than individuals who successfully completed high school to commit crimes (Maynard, Salas-Wright, and Vaughn, 2015; Ou, 2008), abuse drugs and alcohol (Maynard, Salas-Wright, and Vaughn, 2015), have children out of wedlock (Ou, 2008), earn low wages and be un- or underemployed (Autor, Katz, and Kearney, 2008), and suffer poorer health (Owens, 2004; Wolfe and Haveman, 2002; Ou, 2008; Grossman, 2006; Zajacova and Everett, 2014). They also have higher rates of incarceration (Maynard, Salas-Wright, and Vaughn, 2015; Ou, 2008).

There are many programs at the local, state, and federal levels that are aimed at improving the outcomes of young individuals who are at risk or who have dropped out of high school. The National Guard Youth ChalleNGe program (hereafter referred to as ChalleNGe) is a

---

[1]   In the report, these are referred to as the *status dropout rate* and the *average freshman graduation rate*, respectively.

residential, quasi-military program for youths ages 16 to 18 who are experiencing academic difficulties and exhibiting problem behaviors, either inside or outside school; have dropped out or are in jeopardy of dropping out; and, in some cases, have had run-ins with the law. The ChalleNGe program runs for a total of 17.5 months, broken into a 5.5-month Residential Phase (a two-week acclimation period called Pre-ChalleNGe and five-month ChalleNGe), followed by a 12-month Post-Residential Phase. Participating states operate the program, which began in the mid-1990s, with supporting federal funds and oversight from state National Guard organizations. As of early 2020, there were 39 sites in 28 states, the District of Columbia, and Puerto Rico. More than 220,000 young people have taken part in the ChalleNGe program, and nearly 165,000 have completed the program.

The goal of ChalleNGe is to intervene in the lives of participants, called cadets, to change their trajectory and improve their long-term outcomes. Although there are many variations across ChalleNGe sites, each follows and implements a curriculum around the program's eight core components: academic excellence, life coping skills, job skills, health and hygiene, responsible citizenship, service to the community, leadership/followership, and physical fitness. The ChalleNGe program has been previously evaluated in a randomized controlled trial (RCT), in which sites that had more applicants than slots in the program randomized admissions and compared over multiple years those individuals who had been invited to ChalleNGe and those who had not. The RCT was based on ten sites during 2005 and 2006 and conducted follow-up surveys for three years following program exit. The evaluation found that ChalleNGe completers had higher educational attainment and earnings than individuals who did not attend the program. Using these differences, it has been estimated that ChalleNGe is a cost-effective program (see Bloom, Gardenhire-Crooks, and Mandsager, 2009; Millenky, Bloom, and Dillon, 2010; Millenky, Bloom, Muller-Ravett, et al., 2011; Perez-Arce et al., 2012).

Yet, the successful RCT evaluation of the ChalleNGe program—and the validation of the ChalleNGe model—still leaves questions for individual sites about their own success. There are many ways in which a site's cadets may differ from the average cadet, or the average cadet from the RCT participants of a decade ago. Moreover, within ChalleNGe, there is considerable variation across sites in institutional settings, constraints, and goals (see Wenger et al., 2019, for the most recent review of sites). At the same time, all ChalleNGe sites collect data on their incoming cadets and follow their graduates for a 12-month period. Although sites can and do look for trends in their own site over time through these data, they do not have a way to benchmark their progress toward a set of expected outcomes.

Objective of This Report

The objective of this report is to provide ChalleNGe sites with a set of population benchmarks with which to compare their cadets. We build the benchmarks around three groups of individuals, to which we refer as the benchmark groups: high school dropouts who do not attain a GED or equivalent credential, high school dropouts who attain GEDs, and high school graduates who did not attend college. These groups are meant to provide a reasonable comparison group for cadets who have dropped out of high school, but who come to ChalleNGe to attain a GED or to recover credits and reenroll in high school.

We compare these three benchmark groups in two time periods: around the time of dropping out and in the years following. These snapshots can be used to compare the groups at enrollment in ChalleNGe (the preperiod) and a after ChalleNGe is completed (the postperiod), respectively. For the preperiod, we examine and discuss the differences among the three groups. This discussion is meant to inform site directors of how their participant populations differ from the overall population of dropouts, GED holders, and graduates and, in doing so, help site directors identify unique challenges or obstacles present among participants at their site. This may help inform both site-specific policy and expectations of how participants will fare after the program. For the postperiod, we compare the benchmark groups at ages 17 and older. This discussion is meant to help directors interpret the data they collect from 12-month follow-ups with cadets. In that sense, the outcomes of high school dropouts can be thought of as the *expected* outcome, and the outcomes for high school graduates can be thought of as the *successful* outcome. Achievement above a high school diploma we deem an unreasonable expectation. That does not mean that achievement above that is impossible but that setting the expectation that high is unrealistic.

In the rest of this chapter, we discuss the findings from previous literature on factors associated with individuals dropping out of high school and the expected long-term outcomes associated with being a dropout. We then present, given that high school dropouts come from more challenging backgrounds with worse expectations, how intervention programs targeted at dropouts have been evaluated in the past and the need for additional benchmarking. We conclude the chapter by discussing the methodological approach for development of these benchmarks.

Prior Research on High School Dropouts

Intervention programs targeted at high school dropouts, such as ChalleNGe, often have participants who come from more difficult home, community, and school environments and, at least statistically, have worse prospects. Before discussing this in detail, however, we define in Box 1.1 a set of terms that are sometimes used interchangeably with dropout—*at-risk youth*, *disconnected youth*, and *opportunity youth*—both in the literature and in targeting recruits for intervention programs. These terms vary in whether they describe an individual's credentials, characteristics, or current status, but the individuals included in each group are often overlapping.

Dropping Out of High School

There is a long and robust literature that has contributed to our understanding of why certain students do not complete high school. First, studies are in agreement that dropping out should be characterized not as a single event but as a process that typically begins well before high school. Most students show identifiable warning signs several years before they drop out (see, e.g., Allensworth, 2005; Neild and Balfanz,

Box 1.1
Glossary of Terms

High school dropout	Describes credential	Individual of any age who does not have a high school diploma; dropouts who attain a high school–equivalent credential are sometimes still regarded as dropouts.
At-risk youth ("Glossary of Education Reform," undated; "Serving At-Risk Youth," undated; Moore, 2006)	Describes individual and family characteristics	Youth who are likely to experience difficulty in completing high school and are at risk of dropping out, for reasons spanning homelessness, drug use, physical or mental abuse, mental health disorders, family instability, family income, or other factors not necessarily related to intellectual ability.
Disconnected youth (Measure of America, undated; "Reconnecting Youth," undated; Issuelab, undated)	Describes current status	Youth 16 to 24 years old who are neither employed nor enrolled in school. Some definitions expand this to 14 to 24 years old and include youth who are homeless, in foster care, or in the justice system. Some definitions require that disconnected youth not have a high school diploma.
Opportunity youth ("Opportunity Youth Service Initiative," undated; "Who Are Opportunity Youth?" undated)	Describes current status	Youth 16 to 24 years old who are neither employed nor enrolled in school but are not necessarily high school dropouts.

2006; Rumberger, 2004). Second, while the risk factors identified in the literature are manifold and multifaceted (Hammond et al., 2007), not much is known about how these factors interact or about their particular roles in different environments (Ripamonti, 2017). Third, we refer throughout to individuals who drop out of high school, but this encompasses both *early leavers*—those who choose to drop out—and those who *fail to complete* high school, two distinct concepts. This brief review focuses on listing the most widely accepted dropout correlates across different domains. We refrain from providing a detailed discussion about how these correlates interact or how they might influence the decision to drop out. We use the term *correlates*, rather than *determinants* or *indicators*, to be clear that none of the correlates we discuss provides the reason, or cause, of dropping out; instead, each is a characteristic or feature seen in many dropouts.

According to the literature,[2] the most important *demographic correlates* of dropping out include being male, being a member of a racial or ethnic minority, immigrant status, and being older than the average student in one's grade (Allensworth, 2005; Roderick, 1994; Rumberger, 2004; Byrne, McCoy, and Watson, 2008). While the incidence of dropping out is higher among males, female students who become pregnant also are at risk of leaving school prematurely (Marcotte, 2013). Teen parenting, for both males and females, is one of several early adulthood responsibilities that have been found to be associated with a higher likelihood of dropout.

Many studies have discovered a strong relationship between the dropout rate and poverty (see, e.g., Balfanz and Letgers, 2004), family socioeconomic status (e.g., Pong and Ju, 2000), and related *socioeconomic correlates*. The socioeconomic correlates span the student's family and the student's community. Students who do not complete high school are much more likely to come from very-low- or low-income families; lower socioeconomic status has been found to be a strong risk factor in dropping out (Suh and Suh, 1999). At the same time, newer research indicates that other variables may mediate such links; better individual health can mitigate the correlation between socioeconomic status and dropping out (Sznitman, Reisel, and Khurana, 2017). Family structure is also associated with dropping out. As shown in a review by Hammond et al. (2007), students from single-parent and stepparent

---

[2] This is but a small sample of the wealth of literature on dropout correlates. For more discussion, see broad surveys of the literature by Rosenthal (1998), Hammond et al. (2007), and Ripamonti (2017). For dropout prevention strategies, see the meta-analysis by Chappell et al. (2015).

families have been found to be more likely to drop out of school in several studies, as are students whose families move frequently (Brennan and Anderson, 1990; Pittman, 1991). In addition, higher dropout rates have also been identified in communities that have a high incidence of violence, arson, and drug-related crime (Fine, 1986; Bowen and Bowen, 1999); communities that are low income (Stedman et al., 1988); and communities that have high occurrence of the family types correlated with dropouts, such as female-headed households (Brennan and Anderson, 1990).

In terms of *academic performance correlates*, low attendance and poor grades are among the key signs of a student's subsequently dropping out of high school (see, e.g., Allensworth, 2005, Roderick, 1994). Overall, poor academic performance appears to be one of the most consistent correlates of dropout, however measured, and was also often brought up in surveys by dropouts themselves (see, e.g., Bridgeland, Dilulio, and Morison, 2006). School-related factors may mitigate such relationships. Studies considered in a review by Ripamonti (2017), for instance, indicate that students are less likely to drop out when they attend small or medium-sized schools and when they have a low to medium number of classmates. Other individual characteristics found to be linked to leaving school early include limited cognitive abilities and different types of disabilities, both physical and mental. Students who have learning disabilities are particularly vulnerable to dropping out (Hammond et al., 2007; Ripamonti, 2017).

Adolescents may also have "high-risk" attitudes, such as low occupational and educational aspirations, or early antisocial behavior, such as violent behavior or trouble with the law, which several studies (as reviewed in Hammond et al., 2007) have found to be associated with a student's dropping out of high school. The association between high school dropout and attitudes, such as motivation or investment in school activities, seems very robust both in international studies (e.g., Cabus and De Witte, 2016; Lamote et al., 2013) and U.S.-focused literature (e.g., Wang and Fredricks, 2014). These attributes are often related to adult engagement and expectations. Several studies suggest that both teacher expectations and parental involvement can influence students' likelihood of dropping out (Bridgeland, Dilulio, and Balfanz,

2009; Bridgeland, Dilulio, and Morison, 2006; Kaufman, Bradbury, and Owings, 1992; White and Kelly, 2010). Peer groups naturally matter in the decision to drop out as well. Among other results, students who perceive themselves as bullied or harassed appear to be at a higher risk of dropping out (Cornell et al., 2013). Positive relations with friends can, on the other hand, play a protective role (Mahoney, 2014).

Finally, while his paper is not discussed here in detail, Ripamonti (2017, pp. 6–7) surveyed a broad international literature linking the decision to drop out to poor health status, psychological well-being, and substance abuse, finding that all three are strong correlates. Townsend, Flisher, and King (2007) surveyed peer-reviewed empirical articles from 1990 to 2006 and found a consistent relationship between dropping out and chronic substance use.

Many dropouts elect to earn a high school equivalent such as the GED credential rather than graduate from high school.[3] In 2013, the credential was obtained by 541,000 people; for comparison, there were around 3.5 million high school graduates that year (NCES, 2018). Survey data indicate that some high school students drop out early precisely because they feel that it would be easier to obtain a GED (Institute of Education Sciences and U.S. Department of Education, 2011), and the credential may induce some would-be graduates to drop out (Humphries, 2010). The role and effect of the GED has been widely debated and studied since it was first introduced in 1942.

Outcomes for High School Dropouts
Building on some of the related literature, this brief review focuses on the differences in a variety of early adulthood outcomes between high school dropouts, graduates, and GED recipients.[4] There is abundant evidence showing that higher educational attainment leads to eco-

---

[3] See Tyler (2005) for a detailed description of the history of the GED credential. Note also that in official statistics, students with a high school equivalent credential, such as the GED, are considered to have *completed* high school, whereas high school *graduation* refers to students who graduate with a regular diploma.

[4] Prior research often compares dropouts to graduates without the same restrictions we set in defining the benchmark groups—dropouts and GED holders are conflated, and gradu-

nomic success for individuals and benefits the society at large. The positive relationship between education and earnings is well established in the literature (see, e.g., Angrist and Krueger, 1991; Card, 1999), and more recent research has identified a range of social or nonmarket benefits of more education—for example, by improving health and raising living standards (Owens, 2004; Wolfe and Haveman, 2002; Ou, 2008; Grossman, 2006; Zajacova and Everett, 2014). For economic outcomes, there is also evidence that educational attainment is becoming *more important*. As documented by Autor, Katz, and Kearney (2008) and others, since the early 1970s, the real wages of high school dropouts have declined, while those of more-educated workers have risen sharply.

The focus of prior studies comparing these groups has been largely on labor market outcomes. Most studies conclude that GED recipients and high school dropouts fare worse in the labor market than traditional high school graduates in terms of wage and employment outcomes (Heckman, Humphries, and Mader, 2010; Heckman and LaFontaine, 2006; Tyler, 2003; Tyler, 2005; Cameron and Heckman, 1993). Even with their equivalent credential, GED recipients fare worse than graduates on all measures of labor market success, including hourly wages, annual earnings, and the probability of employment.

Slightly different but complementary findings emerge from other studies that focus on comparisons between GED holders and uncredentialed dropouts. Some researchers have found notable differences in subsequent earnings between the two groups, meaning that GED recipients typically fall between graduates and dropouts in earnings and other measures of labor market success (Boudett, Murnane, and Willett, 2000; Maloney, 1991; Clark and Jaeger, 2006).

In addition to economic outcomes, earlier research concerned differences in education and training outcomes among the three groups, most notably participation in postsecondary education and the timing of the completion of secondary degrees. In their research comparing receiving with not receiving the GED, Jepsen, Mueser, and Troske

---

ates who go on to college are included. The numeric findings from this research are not directly comparable with ours.

(2017) found that the credential increased the likelihood of postsecondary attendance and course completion and led to modest gains in credits completed. However, the literature indicates that GED holders had worse postsecondary education outcomes than those with a high school diploma. The GED is generally accepted as a prerequisite for college admission. Although relatively few GED recipients enroll in and graduate from four-year colleges (Heckman, Humphries, and Mader, 2010), some evidence suggests that, in terms of first-time college entry, GED recipients catch up with traditional high school graduates in their 20s despite being less likely to enter college in their late teens (Maralani, 2011). GED recipients who enter college are more likely, on average, to enter a two-year college than a four-year college and complete postsecondary degrees later than those who hold a high school diploma (Maralani, 2006).

Some studies have examined nonmarket outcomes among the three groups. Ou (2008) studied a variety of outcomes among inner-city youths, including incarceration, childbearing, and life satisfaction. She identified a "gradient" in which most of the related outcomes for high school dropouts were worse than those for GED recipients among her population, who, in turn, fared considerably worse than high school graduates did. Relying on a community sample of 585 people followed from ages 5 to 27, Lansford et al. (2016) found similar differences between high school dropouts and graduates. Dropouts were up to four times more likely to experience individual negative outcomes (be arrested, fired, or on government assistance; use illicit substances; or have poor health) by the age of 27 and 24 times more likely to experience four or more of such negative outcomes. Accordingly, Liem, Lustig, and Dillon (2010) found that, in their samples of 1,325 emerging adults, dropouts were much more depressed and reported lower life satisfaction than graduates at the time of their expected graduation. These differences were, however, not statistically significant four years later.

Other researchers have compared health behaviors among graduates, dropouts, and GED recipients. Notably, using data from the 1997 to 2009 National Health Interview Surveys, Zajacova and Everett (2014) analyzed general health among the three groups. They concluded that GED recipients' health was generally comparable to that of high school dropouts and that both groups had worse health outcomes than those with a high school diploma. Graduates have also been found to have lower rates of smoking than GED earners, who are, in turn, only marginally less likely to smoke than dropouts (Kenkel, Lillard, and Mathios, 2006; Ou, 2008). Substance abuse has been reported to be more frequent among GED recipients than among high school graduates (Ou, 2008), while no statistically significant differences have been found in being overweight (Kenkel, Lillard, and Mathios, 2006). Collectively, the studies suggest that most nonmarket outcomes for an average GED recipient are considerably worse than corresponding outcomes for an average graduate and, typically, comparable to those for dropouts.

Program Evaluations of Intervention Programs Aimed at High School Dropouts

The basic goal of intervention programs aimed at high school dropouts—programs targeting those who have already dropped out, as opposed to those aiming to prevent dropout—is to improve on the outcomes previously discussed. However, the target population for program participants—high school dropouts—comes from more-difficult home, community, and school environments and, at least statistically, had worse prospects than individuals who did not drop out of school. This makes it difficult to identify positive effects. Nonetheless, it is vital to measure a program's effectiveness, ensuring both that participants enrolled in a program are getting the best supports and help and that funders' (often taxpayers') money is properly spent.

Evaluations, however, are difficult. The challenge common to virtually all intervention programs, regardless of the populations they target, is that the pool of participants is not random, even within the target population. Individuals must meet certain eligibility criteria; programs often have discretion over how to target their recruitment efforts; and participation is voluntary. Thus, individuals choose to apply and, if admitted, choose to enroll. Critically, those choices are a function of important characteristics of these individuals, whether positive, such as motivation and discipline, or negative, such as an unstable home environment that they are willing to leave. Youth ChalleNGe participants, for example, are not a random sample of the population of high school dropouts. They select to enroll in a quasi-military program in which they live away from their families for nearly six months. Their preference to do this reflects certain characteristics; those characteristics set them apart from the overall population of youths and even from the overall population of high school dropouts. Given choices and characteristics that result in voluntary participation in a program, it is difficult to detect whether that program changes the short- or long-term outcomes of participants, given that the factors driving individuals to participate may be correlated with those outcomes.

An RCT is the gold standard of program evaluation because it resolves the issue of selection into program participation. Successful applicants to the program are randomized into participation; some will be asked to attend the program, and the rest will not. Those individuals who were and were not asked to participate in the program, respectively, are compared over several years. In this way, any differences in outcomes between the two groups can be attributed to the program. Notably, the groups are defined by whether they were asked to attend the program, not whether they actually attended or completed the program. This is done to avoid selection in program completion; not every participant will complete the program, and comparing only successful participants with all nonparticipants would bias the results. Hence, an RCT consistently estimates the average effect of the *program* on the population randomly assigned when there is perfect compliance within the RCT (i.e., everyone finishes) or consistently estimates the average effect of the *program offer* on the population randomly assigned when there is imperfect compliance (i.e., not everyone starts or finishes the program).[5]

Youth ChalleNGe has been evaluated using an RCT (Millenky, Bloom, Muller-Ravett, et al., 2011), as have two other large federal programs aimed at dropout or disconnected youth: Job Corps (Scho-

---

[5]   In cases in which some of the invited program participants do not start or finish the program, an RCT can, depending on adjustments, be used to estimate the effect of *program completion on finishers* within the population randomly assigned.

chet, Burghardt, and Glazerman, 2001; Schochet, Burghardt, and McConnell, 2006; Schochet, Burghardt, and McConnell, 2008; Berk et al., 2018) and Youth Build. The ChalleNGe and YouthBuild programs used a subset of sites for the RCT; Job Corps used all sites. For each program, positive effects were found for participants through higher education, higher earnings, or lower incarceration among the treated (participant) group than in the control (nonparticipant) group. The programs varied in how long the follow-up period extended and whether results faded out over that time period. In Table 1.1, we compare program and RCT results of ChalleNGe with those for Job Corps and YouthBuild. Those programs target similar populations, though ChalleNGe draws from a younger population only.

RCTs are a powerful tool in validating program design. They provide causal evidence that a program improves outcomes and provide estimates of program benefits. Those benefits can then be compared with program cost, enabling an estimate of the cost-effectiveness of the program. For example, Youth ChalleNGe was found to generate $2.66 in economic benefit for every $1 spent (Perez-Arce et al., 2012), given the cost of the program and the difference in expected earnings for participants. The Job Corps and YouthBuild RCTs were the basis of similar estimates of the net-benefit return to society. In general, cost-benefit estimates expressed as a single number require a lot of calculating assumptions, such as how many years after the program the return to society or the economy is calculated. Rather than placing too much emphasis on the specific dollar amount, the observer should glean that the RCT enabled a major justification of the program by showing that there is a return to society through higher earnings.

However, relying on the RCT results may not be sufficient evaluation for a program's site directors. The RCT's validation of the overall program model does not validate the performance of every specific site or the policies deployed within sites. And site policies may change in response to changing participant population, changing staff, or changing funding opportunities (Wenger et al., 2019). Moreover, RCTs include special follow-up surveys designed specifically for the RCT evaluation; sites cannot easily generate comparable statistics to assess their graduates in relation to the RCT's findings. In other words, while

Table 1.1
Features of Three Federally Funded Youth Intervention Programs

Feature	Youth ChalleNGe	Job Corps	YouthBuild
Eligible population	16- to 18-year-olds without a high school diploma and who do not have a felony record	16–24-year-olds who are low income and meet at least one of these criteria: (1) skills deficient; (2) high school dropout; (3) homeless, runaway, or aged out of foster care; (4) parent; (5) human trafficking victim; (6) in need of employment training	16–24-year-old high school dropouts who are low income, in foster care, or disabled; have criminal records; are children of incarcerated, or are migrants
Federal funder	National Guard	Department of Labor	Department of Labor
Number of sites	39	125	187
Participants per year (estimate)	12,000	60,000	8,000
Program structure	5.5-month residential program in which youth live on National Guard bases and take educational classes in highly structured, quasi-military setting	Self-paced residential program, lasting eight months to two years, in which youth live at Job Corps centers and take a mix of education and employment classes	Ten-month program in which youth remain at home and take a mix of education classes, employment training, and construction projects
RCT	Conducted in 2005–2008; found an increase in educational attainment and employment and reduction in criminal activity	Conducted in 2001–2008; found an increase in wages and in educational attainment and a reduction in arrests, though some of the longer follow-ups found that the control group caught up to the treated (Job Corps) group	Conducted in 2010–2016, ongoing; found an increase in educational attainment and increase in vocational training

SOURCES: For Job Corps, Job Corps (undated); Schochet, Burghardt, and McConnell (2008) (RCT). For YouthBuild, "About YouthBuild USA" (2019); Miller et al. (2016) (RCT). For Youth ChalleNGe, Wenger et al. (2019); Millenky, Bloom, Muller-Ravett et al., (2011) (RCT); Perez-Arce et al. (2012).

NOTE: The participant estimate includes those who did not complete the program.

the cost-effectiveness estimate from the RCT can help with recruiting, a trial comparing three-year-out earning differences, and, as in ChalleNGe's case, at a subset of sites will not necessarily inform site directors that their own site and the new policies or practices that they are pursuing would be as successful, many years after the RCT evaluation has completed, and potentially many states away.

Methodological Approach of This Research

As we discussed in the previous section, the literature has established that high school dropouts tend to struggle more in school with academics, absences, and discipline and that they come from more difficult family situations and communities. After leaving, they are expected to fare worse in terms of economic outcomes, family outcomes, and even health outcomes. However, the literature also indicates that, despite this, intervention programs, including ChalleNGe, can make improvements in long-term outcomes.

The aim of this report is to bridge the gap between these two strands of the literature in a way that is practical and useful for ChalleNGe site directors. We establish a set of population benchmarks to inform site directors in developing expectations of reasonable outcomes for their program participants. Rather than establish a control group and follow its members over time, as is done in an RCT, we instead devise a set of population averages that site directors can use as a reasonable comparison with their Youth ChalleNGe participants at any time. In this way, our benchmarks can help site directors and staff on the ground gauge their own site's performance. We provide a framework for interpreting long-term outcomes that delineates between expected outcomes and successful outcomes and, in the process, identifies unrealistic outcomes.

Our means of doing this is to create comparison groups for ChalleNGe participants. As we noted previously, a key obstacle in evaluating a program is selection into program participation. An RCT solves this by pooling successful applicants and randomizing their participation. We solve this by analyzing three populations that represent the scope of potential selection for ChalleNGe: high school dropouts who do not get an equivalent credential (we refer to these as *dropouts*); high school dropouts who do get an equivalent credential (we refer to these as *GED holders*); and high school graduates who never attend college (we refer to these as *graduates*). These groups should not be thought of as *good* and *bad* populations or *starting* and *goal* populations; they are meant to represent the potential set of ChalleNGe participants and span what we refer to as the *spectrum of selection*. We discuss each group in detail below.

High School Dropouts

We define *high school dropout* as someone who indicates that they hold neither a high school diploma nor an equivalent by a certain time or age (it varies by survey, which we discuss in detail in Chapter Two). In our benchmarks, dropouts nearly always provide the lower bound for good outcomes and the upper bound for bad outcomes. It is important to note that it is likely that even individuals in this group—namely, those who do not attain an educational credential—could have been involved in some sort of intervention program, either within school or outside of school. For example, the ChalleNGe RCT evaluation found that 30 percent of those individuals asked to participate in ChalleNGe had neither a high school diploma nor its equivalent three years after the program. These results could be attributed to individuals who did not enroll in or complete the program, but even participants do not leave with a credential in all cases. Hence, it is inaccurate to think of high school dropouts as "untreated," in the strictest sense, or the "starting" group from which to improve. As we say in the goal for defining groups, dropouts reflect one part of the spectrum of selection of ChalleNGe participants.

GED Holders

We define *high school equivalent holder* as someone who obtains an alternative credential, either the GED or the High School Equivalency Test (known as the HiSET) by a specific age. Because the GED is more common, we refer to it throughout, though the credential itself could be the result of either exam. The age by which a GED is awarded varies and is determined by the structure of the survey. In the Current Population Survey (CPS), high school equivalent holders must have a GED by the time of the survey and can be anywhere in age from 14 to 24; in the National Longitudinal Survey of Youth (NLSY), they must have a GED by age 28; and, in the Education Longitudinal Study (ELS), by age 27. Given that each participant obtaining a GED is the goal of many youth dropout intervention programs, including GED holders as a separate category, rather than folded into dropouts or graduates, is useful for setting benchmarks ranges. GED holders in public surveys display two key traits that make them reasonably comparable to program participants: First, they have dropped out of high school, and second, they have completed a voluntary credential. In other words, they represent a different part of the spectrum of selection.

High School Graduates Without Any Postsecondary Enrollment

The final group is high school graduates who, by the same ages as those for GED attainment, have not attended a postsecondary institution. We excluded high school graduates who attended college (whether two year or four year), though we did not exclude GED holders who attended college. In constructing groups to constitute the benchmark estimates, our aim was to represent the potential set of ChalleNGe participants. Individuals with a high school diploma who attend college differ in key ways from those who graduate and do not attend and from those who get an equivalency and later attend. As we noted earlier in the chapter, the college student with a high school diploma is more likely to come from a higher-income family, less likely to be from a single-parent household, have higher grades, and have one or more parents who graduated from college. Hence, we determined that comparing outcomes of those individuals was unreasonable for ChalleNGe and that, even with positive selection into ChalleNGe, high school graduates who attend college were beyond the spectrum of selection.

Organization of This Report

We discuss our sources of data in detail in Chapter Two, the preperiod analyses in Chapter Three, and the postperiod analyses in Chapter Four. We end in Chapter Five with a discussion and key takeaway figures. Throughout the report, we focus our analysis and our discussion on the ChalleNGe program. Although our findings are broadly usable by directors of the other multisite programs in Table 1.1 or of other youth intervention programs, our analysis is intended for use by ChalleNGe site directors.

CHAPTER TWO

Data Sources

We used three publicly available datasets to establish our benchmarks. In this chapter, we describe those sources and the methods used to identify high school dropouts, GED holders, and high school graduates who did not enroll in postsecondary education.

Current Population Survey, October Supplements, 1996–2016

The CPS is a monthly survey conducted by the U.S. Census Bureau to collect information about employment, unemployment, earnings, income, and other attributes of the U.S. population. The Census Bureau surveys around 60,000 households every month. Surveyed households are filtered through rotation groups; each household spends four months in the survey, followed by eight months out of the survey, and then four months back in the survey. Hence, the CPS is a cross-sectional survey, because new households are added to the sample each month as other households leave, but it is also a two-period panel survey, since each household is interviewed in the same month over two years.

In October of each year, the CPS supplements the usual survey questions (referred to as the Core Questionnaire) with additional questions pertaining to school enrollment and educational attainment, with the majority of questions aimed at respondents ages 3 to 24. The October supplement allows us to identify our benchmark groups. Although the Core Questionnaire measures educational attainment, as do most household surveys, it does not separately measure GED or other equivalent versus high school diploma. The October supplement has additional questions about the type of high school credential. Hence, we use the 1996 to 2016 October waves of the CPS in our study of dropouts. We select those years because 1996 roughly corresponds to the start of the ChalleNGe program, and 2016 is the most recent year of available data. For our analysis, we use the CPS in two ways. First, we use the linked, year-over-year observations to identify dropouts at the time they are leaving school. This supports the analysis in Chapter Three and spans individuals who are 14 to 21, though 95 percent of dropouts we identify in the CPS are younger than 19.[1] Then, we use the unlinked data to examine the outcomes of all three benchmark groups—dropouts, GED holders, and graduates—after they have left school. This supports the analysis in Chapter Four and spans individuals who are 19 to 24.

First CPS Sample Used for This Study—Linked at Time of Dropout
An individual is a dropout if they are observed to be enrolled in school the first year observed and not enrolled (and not a graduate) in the second year observed. Other than the supplement age maximum of 24, we did not put any age limits or restrictions on identifying dropouts but built our sample based on individuals who were enrolled in grades 9 through 12 in the first survey. Using year-over-year observations, we could identify both dropouts and the grade in which they dropped out. We defined the dropout grade as the last grade of school in which the student had been enrolled. We examined all grades 9 through 12. For the 20 years of survey waves, we created a sample of individuals who were enrolled in high school in the first year they were observed in the survey and observed for two consecutive years.[2]

---

[1]   The data are obtained from the linked CPS files from the *Integrated Public Use Microdata Series* (Flood et al., 2017). We drop any observations in which the respondent is not observed twice, and cases in which age, sex, or race of the respondent conflict. Notes on how linking is constructed and what accounts for errors is discussed in Rivera Drew, Flood, and Warren, 2014.

[2]   This truncates the total sample in the first (1996) and last (2016) waves; half of the 1996 sample started the prior year, and half of the 2016 sample ended the following year.

Our sample comprised 69,941 respondents. Of these, we observed that 2,740 individuals dropped out of school between observations, a dropout rate of 3.9 percent.

This dropout rate of 3.9 percent is slightly lower than the CPS Indicator of Event Dropout produced by the NCES in its annual report on the trends in high school dropout and completion rates (McFarland, Cui, and Stark, 2018). However, the NCES definition is more restrictive than ours. To be included in the NCES measure, an individual has to be enrolled in grade 10, 11, or 12 at the first observation and not enrolled and not credentialed at the second observation. Our measure is broader: To be included, an individual has to be enrolled in grade 9, 10, 11, or 12 at the first observation and not enrolled and not credentialed at the second observation. The NCES measure is the share of students who begin high school but do not finish, while ours is a measure of the share of students who do not finish high school. Because dropout rates are relatively low in the two younger grades, our rate is lower. The NCES Indicator of Event Dropout from the CPS is designed to be comparable to other indicators collected in the NCES analysis. Without that restriction, we examine a broader set of dropouts. Our motivation in doing so was the ChalleNGe program. ChalleNGe participants are 16 to 18 years old and are not currently enrolled in high school—there is no restriction on when or at what grade they left, and, in fact, in the RCT evaluation of ChalleNGe, around 45 percent of ChalleNGe participants had left school before grade 10.[3]

One benefit of the CPS is that it has a large sample; we can compare how dropouts' characteristics vary by the final grade attended before they dropped out. Another benefit is that the CPS is a household dataset—data are collected about each member of the household. The dropout's parents, if they are in the household, are also in the survey. That allows us to describe the economic and demographic characteristics of the student and the parents.

---

[3]   See Millenky, Bloom, Muller-Ravett, et al., 2011, Table 2, "Selected Characteristics of ChalleNGe Survey Sample Members at the Time of Random Assignment (Column 3)."

Second CPS Sample Used for This Study—Observed After Age 18

Because the October supplement is fielded to all individuals ages 3 through 24, there is a large number of individuals whom we observed after the traditional high school age and for whom we know detailed educational attainment. We constructed a sample of dropouts, GED holders, and high school graduates based on their status in the second year of observation. For this method, we do not use the linked observations in any way. Over the 20 years of survey waves, we observed 56,175 individuals ages 19 through 24 for whom we could measure educational attainment. Of these, 4,343 are high school dropouts, 2,304 are GED holders, and 12,179 are high school graduates who had not enrolled in college. It is important to point out that the classification into one of these groups is age dependent. That is, an individual observed in the CPS is a dropout, GED holder, or graduate at the time they were observed in the survey. It is possible that they could change groups as they get older if they attain their GED or decide to (re)enroll in school. In the other data sources, this is not a concern, but it is for the CPS.

The advantages to using the CPS are that it is a large, staid household dataset with high response rates; low attrition; a core data set of employment, demographics, and income; and a supplement that allows identification of our benchmark groups. The drawbacks to the CPS are that the core questions, and even the October supplement, have little depth about the experiences of youths as they near high school completion. For this reason, we used two additional datasets in our benchmark analysis.

National Longitudinal Survey of Youth, 1997 Cohort

The NLSY comprises a family of panel datasets that follow a set of young individuals over time.[4] The 1997 NLSY is a household survey

---

[4]   The first NLSY started with 12,600 respondents who were ages 14 to 22 in 1979 (born from 1957 through 1965) and surveyed annually or biennially since. Up to 26 waves of data have been collected on the 1979 cohort. In addition, a new panel was started in 1986 comprising the children of the female respondents of the 1979 cohort, called the NLSY Chil-

that was designed to be representative of the population born from 1980 through 1984. It consists of a cross-sectionally representative sample of 6,700 respondents and a supplemental oversample of 2,200 black and Hispanic respondents.[5] The 9,000 respondents were 12 to 17 years old when first surveyed in 1997. They have since been interviewed 17 times on an annual, and now biennial, basis. In the most recent publicly available wave fielded in 2013, members of the cohort were 28 to 33 years old. The NLSY is a rich dataset that collects information on both outcomes and behavior related to education, income, employment, dating and sexual activity, health, and crime; characteristics of the family, neighborhood, and living conditions of the respondent; and attitudes and beliefs.

The NLSY Sample Used for This Study

For our analysis, we defined our three benchmark groups by their educational attainment status at age 28. Hence, we could compare individuals at earlier ages, before dropping out or attaining the GED or finishing high school, while still knowing in which group they would end up. This is the advantage of a longitudinal study like the NLSY over the larger cross-section of the CPS. The trade-off is the smaller sample: The NLSY has 1,000 high school dropouts, 1,127 GED holders, and 1,507 graduates who have never attended college. In Chapter Three, we discuss the NLSY sample at age 16, and, in Chapter Four, we discuss the NLSY sample from ages 19 to 28. The NLSY has an oversample of the black and Hispanic populations; we included this oversample and adjusted with appropriate weights to maintain the sample's representativeness of the population. The NLSY interviews incarcerated panel members—something that the ELS and the CPS do not do. To make the samples more comparable, we dropped the currently incarcerated from the NLSY.

---

dren and Young Adult sample. By the 2014 wave, this sample included over 11,000 children observed for up to 15 waves. Given lessons learned between the two prior cohorts, a new cohort, unrelated to the first two, was started in 1997. We use this cohort for our analysis.

[5] For more information on NLSY sampling weights, see National Longitudinal Surveys (1997).

One drawback of the NLSY is that, although there are numerous household and individual characteristics that provide an in-depth comparison of youths who do and do not finish school, the survey has less information on academics and schooling outcomes. For that reason, we used a third dataset that focuses on academics.

The Education Longitudinal Study of 2002

The ELS 2002 is, like the NLSY, one of a family of longitudinal datasets. Each dataset tracks a set of students with periodic follow-ups and collects in-depth academic information while the respondents are in school and then follows up as the respondents age and enter the labor market. The ELS 2002 is the most recent of these studies.[6]

The ELS 2002 is a nationally representative survey of tenth-graders in 2002. The majority were born in 1985 or 1986, meaning that members of the ELS sample were a couple of years younger than those in the 1997 NLSY sample. To generate a grade-representative sample, the ELS started by selecting 750 schools and then sampled a random set of tenth-graders within those schools. The ELS interviews teachers, parents, and school administrators; collects transcripts; and administers academic tests to the sample. The initial ELS cohort was followed up in 2004, when the students (if still in school) were seniors, and in 2006 and 2012. Like the NLSY, the ELS is a rich dataset, with numerous measures of academic performance and achievement, in addition to similar demographic, family, and neighborhood characteristics. We are able to compare our three benchmark groups across the two surveys along similar metrics.

The ELS Sample Used for This Study
As we did with the NLSY, we defined our three benchmark groups in the ELS by their educational attainment status at the third follow-up in

---

[6]   Other datasets in the ELS family are the National Longitudinal Study of the Class of 1972, the High School and Beyond study of 1980, and the National Education Longitudinal Study of 1988.

2012, when the sample members were 26 to 27 years old. In the ELS, we identified 761 high school dropouts, 754 GED holders, and 3,442 high school graduates who did not attend college. In Chapter Three, we discuss the ELS sample in tenth grade, and, in Chapter Four, we discuss the 2006 and 2012 follow-ups, when the sample members were 21 and 27.

Comparisons Across the Samples

Our three samples are not perfectly comparable across the benchmark groups. The CPS defines the groups by educational attainment at the age of observation, while the NLSY and ELS define the groups by attainment at a later age (27 or 28). The CPS and the NLSY identify high school dropouts at any age or grade, while the ELS can identify only those who were enrolled up to at least tenth grade. The samples also pull from different birth years. Table 2.1 summarizes the three samples and the comparison concerns; for each sample, we use provided sample weights.

Neither of the surveys or samples within surveys is without drawbacks in discussing benchmarks for ChalleNGe. For example, the CPS has a large sample with more-recent dropouts (observed dropping out as late as 2016), compared with individuals in the NLSY, who are now in their 30s. However, the CPS does not follow individuals for more than one year and can differentiate graduates from GED holders for only a portion of the sample, and only up to age 24. On the other hand, the CPS and the NLSY include individuals who drop out before the tenth grade, while the ELS does not—but, as we noted earlier, up to 45 percent of ChalleNGe participants in the earlier RCT evaluation reported leaving school before tenth grade. However, the ELS contains rich information about academics, scholastic achievement, and participation that the NLSY does not, which is critical for understanding a key component of dropping out.

We note throughout the report when these sample or survey differences are relevant to our comparisons and, in particular, to discussing ChalleNGe.

Table 2.1
Summary of Data Sources and Sample Comparison Concerns

Sample Characteristic	CPS Linked Observations (Ages 14–19)	CPS Status (Ages 19–24)	NLSY	ELS
Year of birth	1977–2002	1973–1997	1980–1984	1985–1986
Sample representativeness	The CPS sample is nationally representative of all households in the United States (of all ages) and excludes institutionalized population		Sample is representative of the population born 1980–1984	Sample is representative of all enrolled tenth-graders in 2002
Dropout comparison concerns	Includes dropouts from any grade who remain in the survey in both years, ages 14–19	Individuals who do not have a degree and are not enrolled, ages 19–24	Includes dropouts from any grade	Dropouts needed to have been enrolled in tenth grade
GED comparison concerns	Not measured	Individuals had to have GED at time of survey	Individuals awarded GED by age 28	Individuals awarded GED by age 27
College enrollment concerns	Not measured	Individuals with a high school diploma were not enrolled and had not previously enrolled at the time of the survey	Individuals with a high school diploma had not enrolled in college by age 28	Individuals with a high school diploma had not enrolled in college by age 28

CHAPTER THREE

Benchmarks During the Dropout Period

In this chapter, we compare the three benchmark groups—high school dropouts, GED holders, and high school graduates—around the time of dropping out. This can be thought of as a preintervention comparison. This discussion is meant to inform site directors of how their participant populations differ from the overall population of dropouts, GED holders, and graduates. We frame our discussion around the correlates of dropping out that we discussed in Chapter One: demographic correlates, socioeconomic correlates (which we divide into family and individual characteristics), and academic correlates. Our goal is to add numeric references to the findings in the literature for the benefit of ChalleNGe site directors.

Demographics

The first set of characteristics we discuss is the demographic features of individuals in the benchmark groups—gender, race and ethnicity, and immigrant status. Although we examined all benchmark groups, we first focus on high school dropouts in the year they left school. In Table 3.1, we summarize the characteristics of all individuals whom we observe dropping out in the 1996 to 2016 waves of the October CPS. We arrange the dropouts by the final grade enrolled. The first column shows the average across all dropouts, and the subsequent four show the average by the final grade attended (the grade enrolled in the first October observation). This allows us to compare dropouts based on when they left school.

Table 3.1
Demographic Means of Dropouts in the Year After Leaving School, by Final Grade Attended (CPS)

Demographic Characteristic	All High School Dropouts	9th Grade	10th Grade	11th Grade	12th Grade
Number in sample	2,304	325	484	760	735
Percentage of all dropouts	100	14	21	33	32
Demographic, as a percentage					
Male	58	62	58	56	59
White (non-Hispanic)	49	51	52	51	46
Black (non-Hispanic)	22	24	23	20	21
Hispanic[a]	24	20	21	23	29
Immigrant	11	9	9	10	13
First-generation American	15	16	13	15	16
Does not live with parents	20	20	15	19	23

SOURCES: Data are from the 1996–2016 October supplements of the CPS; supplement weights were used.

NOTE: Dropouts in the CPS are identified by indicating in the initial October survey that they were enrolled and, in the second survey, 12 months later, that they were not enrolled and had not received a diploma. In first column, dropout population is statistically different from nondropout population; in the second through fifth columns, dropout population statistically differs by year of dropout.

[a] Hispanic and white (or black) are not exclusive categories in the CPS, in that white or black is race and Hispanic is ethnicity. We define Hispanic as an ethnic group and remove from the black and white race categories anyone of Hispanic ethnicity, to make the categories mutually exclusive.

As seen in the top row, only 14 percent of dropouts left after starting ninth grade, compared with 21 percent after starting tenth grade, 33 percent for eleventh, and 32 percent for twelfth. Fifty-eight percent of high school dropouts are male; 49 percent are white; 11 percent are immigrants; 15 percent are first-generation Americans (meaning their parents are immigrants); and 20 percent do not live with their parents.

Early dropouts have slightly higher male shares (62 percent), while twelfth-grade dropouts have higher Hispanic and immigrant shares (29 percent and 13 percent, respectively). Otherwise, the demographic characteristics of dropouts are similar regardless of when they left.

The limit to using the CPS is that status as a dropout is captured at the time of the survey. As noted in the previous chapter, the NLSY and the ELS are longitudinal studies that follow cohorts of young Americans over time. Hence, we use educational attainment status at later ages (28 in the NLSY and 27 in the ELS) to identify whether respondents are dropouts, GED holders, or high school graduates who did not attend college by the end of their 20s, and then compare the groups when they were younger. In other words, we can compare individuals before their educational choices were made, knowing the group to which they later belonged.

Table 3.2 compares the demographic characteristics of 16-year-olds in the NLSY (top panel) and tenth graders in the ELS (bottom panel), by benchmark group. The differences between the three groups are statistically significant; we do not show stars for ease of reading. Of the total NLSY sample, 7.4 percent are high school dropouts, 11.6 percent are GED holders, and 16.1 percent are high school graduates who did not enroll in college; we do not compare the remaining 65 percent of the sample who finished traditional high school and attended college at some point. In each of the lower educational attainment categories, males are overrepresented, at 55 percent, 59 percent, and 60 percent for dropouts, GED holders, and graduates, respectively. Compared with high school graduates, dropouts and GED holders are more likely to be black. Black subjects made up 21 percent of dropouts and 23 percent of GED holders, compared with 16 percent of graduates. Hispanic subjects have similar shares among GED holders and graduates, between 14 and 16 percent, but are 21 percent of dropouts.

Of the total ELS sample, the school-based survey, 5.2 percent are high school dropouts, 5.1 percent are GED holders, and 22.2 percent are graduates who did not attend college. This slightly lower rate of dropouts and GED holders is expected because the ELS is conditional on enrolling in the tenth grade—by which point, as shown in the CPS in the previous table, 14 percent of dropouts have already left school.

Table 3.2
Demographic Means of Dropouts, GED Holders, and High School Graduates Who Do Not Enroll in College at Age 16 (NLSY) and Grade 10 (ELS)

Demographic Category	Dropout	GED Holder	High School Graduate
Age 16 in the NLSY			
N (persons)	919	1,134	1,374
Percentage of NLSY sample	7.4%	11.6%	16.1%
Male	55%	59%	60%
White	58%	62%	68%
Black	21%	23%	16%
Hispanic	21%	14%	16%
Grade 10 in the ELS			
N (persons)	761	754	3,442
Percentage of ELS sample	5.2%	5.1%	22.2%
Male	57%	60%	61%
White	39%	53%	56%
Black	24%	17%	15%
Hispanic	29%	19%	18%

NOTE: Members of the 1997 NLSY sample reached age 16 in the 1997–2001 waves, depending on age at sample start. Sample is weighted using the panel weights. The ELS 2002 is a sample of tenth-graders; means are weighted with base-year student weight. The differences between the three groups are statistically significant; we do not show stars for ease of reading.

Because the sample was initiated in the spring of the tenth-grade year of respondents, ELS respondents are not representative of all youths, as in the NLSY, but all enrolled youths. Hence, some sample means are different. Regardless, like the CPS and NLSY, the ELS shows higher shares of male, black, and Hispanic respondents among the dropout and GED groups.

The CPS, NLSY, and ELS are meant to be representative of some part of the population—the CPS of all U.S. households, the NLSY of youths born between 1981 and 1985, and the ELS of tenth-graders in 2002. However, as we discussed in the previous chapter, many at-risk or dropout youth intervention programs, including ChalleNGe, recruit from select parts of the population, even among dropouts. In Table 3.3, we compare the demographic characteristics of dropouts in the three surveys with the characteristics of previous RCT evaluations of youth programs: Youth ChalleNGE, Job Corps, and YouthBuild.

Only Job Corps has the expected male share of the dropout population, at 59 percent, while Youth ChalleNGe (88 percent) and YouthBuild (64 percent) are disproportionately male. This could be attributed to Job Corps making accommodations to young mothers. All the programs, however, are less white and less Hispanic than dropouts overall, with a much higher concentration of black individuals, at 34 percent for Youth ChalleNGe, 48 percent for Job Corps, and 63 percent for YouthBuild. YouthBuild was started as an inner-city program, and both YouthBuild and Job Corps have large numbers of urban program sites. Youth ChalleNGe, on the other hand, tends to have programs located on National Guard or other service installations, and there are more programs in the South than in any other region.

In terms of education, nearly one in five Job Corps participants has a traditional high school diploma, compared with 9 percent of YouthBuild and 0 percent of Youth ChalleNGe. Comparatively, because ChalleNGe is limited to 16- to 18-year-olds, the population has dropped out of school at earlier ages than YouthBuild participants or the average high school dropout in general. Indeed, 83 percent of ChalleNGe participants dropped out of school before eleventh grade.

The demographic differences between the population groups in Tables 3.1 and 3.2 and the intervention program participants in Table 3.3 offer an illustration of how to use this report for ChalleNGe program directors. Cadets are much more male than the average dropout but also drop out in earlier grades, likely indicating that they have greater academic needs. These are features to keep in mind when discussing the remaining characteristics.

Table 3.3
Comparison of CPS, NLSY, and ELS Dropouts with Samples of Previous Studies of Youth Intervention Programs

Demographic Category	CPS (1996–2016)	NLSY (Age 16, 1997–2001)	ELS (Grade 10, 2002)	Youth ChalleNGe[a] (2005)	Job Corps[b] (1995)	YouthBuild[c] (2011)
Number in sample	2,304	997	761	1,713	14,237	3,929
Demographic, as percentage						
Male	58	55	57	88	59	64
White	49	58	39	42	27	15
Black	22	21	24	34	48	63
Hispanic	24	21	29	18	18	15
Educational attainment, as percentage						
High school diploma	0[d]			0	18	9
12th grade	32			0	x	10
11th grade	33			17	x	35
10th grade	21			38	x	26
9th grade	14			30	x	18
Less than 9th grade	0[d]			15	x	9

SOURCES: Data are from the 1996–2016 October supplements of the CPS; supplement weights were used.

NOTE: Dropouts in the CPS are identified by indicating in the initial October survey that they were enrolled and, in the second survey, 12 months later, that they were not enrolled and had not received a diploma.

[a] Millenky, Bloom, Muller-Ravett, et al., 2011, Table 2, "Selected Characteristics of ChalleNGe Survey Sample Members at the Time of Random Assignment," column 3.

[b] Schochet, Burghardt, and McConnell, 2008, Table 1, "Characteristics of Eligible Job Corps Applicants."

[c] Miller et al., 2016, Table 1.2, "Baseline Characteristics of YouthBuild Sample."

[d] In the first column, *high school dropout* is defined as someone who left high school without completing a degree, so these categories are 0% of the sample by definition. "x" indicates that data were not provided in the source table.

Family

We next discuss the characteristics of the families of the benchmark groups. As in the last section, we start by looking only at dropouts in the CPS and compare dropouts by the grade in which they left. Given that ChalleNGe cadets leave high school earlier than the dropouts, we use Table 3.4 as a way to understand whether leaving school earlier or later is correlated with different observable family traits. One benefit of the CPS is that it is a household survey; each member of the household responds to the questionnaire. Thus, if the dropout is living with a parent, the survey collects information about the parent—often much more detailed than that collected in the other two surveys. Again, though, the information is collected *conditional* on having a parent present.

Eighty-four percent of dropouts have a mother in the household, and 27 percent of all observed mothers of dropouts were high school dropouts themselves. Sixty-five percent of those observed mothers are employed, and 31 percent are not in the labor force, meaning that they neither work nor are actively looking for work. Conditional on being employed, 75 percent are employed full time but paid hourly, and 7 percent of observed mothers have variable hours, meaning that they do not work similar numbers of hours week to week. Twelfth-grade dropouts are slightly less likely to have a mother in the household and slightly more likely to have a mother who is a high school dropout. Otherwise, the employment, full-time, and hourly rates are similar, but younger dropouts' mothers have more variable hours.

Only 59 percent of high school dropouts have a father in the household, and 29 percent of observed fathers were high school dropouts. Observed fathers have high employment rates—81 percent are working, and only 14 percent are not in the labor force. Conditional on working, 87 percent work full time, 65 percent are paid hourly, and 9 percent have variable hours. The dropout rate for fathers, like that of mothers, is higher among individuals who left school in twelfth grade, at 34 percent. The employment, full-time status, and hours vary by dropout grade but not with any consistent pattern.

Table 3.4

Means of Family Characteristics of Dropouts in the Year After Leaving School, by Final Grade Attended (CPS)

Family Characteristic	All High School Dropouts (%)	9th Grade (%)	10th Grade (%)	11th Grade (%)	12th Grade (%)
Mother in household	84	83	88	86	81
Mother is a high school dropout	27	26	25	24	31
Mother employed	65	62	60	69	64
Mother full time[a]	75	71	75	72	79
Mother paid hourly	74	80	70	71	76
Mother variable hours[b]	7	9	10	6	6
Mother unemployed	4	4	6	4	3
Mother not in labor force	31	34	33	27	33
Father in household	59	61	60	61	57
Father is a high school dropout	29	28	29	27	34
Father employed	81	85	76	83	82
Father full time[a]	87	84	88	86	88
Father paid hourly	65	76	52	66	65
Father variable hours[b]	9	13	9	8	9
Father unemployed	4	4	1	4	6
Father not in labor force	14	11	21	13	12

SOURCES: Data are from the 1996–2016 October supplements of the CPS; supplement weights were used.

NOTE: Dropouts in the CPS are identified by indicating in the initial October survey that they were enrolled and, in the second survey, 12 months later, that they were not enrolled and had not received a diploma. In first column, dropout population is statistically different from nondropout population; in the second through fifth columns, dropout population statistically differs by year of dropout.

[a] Full-time workers are those who usually work 35 hours or more each week at their main job.

[b] Variable hours is a dummy indicating the respondent's job does not have the same number of hours week to week. The CPS is a roster survey; information about mother and father is collected only if they were in the household.

From this, we conclude that although there are slight differences, there do not appear to be strong associations between the observed parent's education and employment status and the grade in which individuals drop out of school.

In Table 3.5, we compare the family characteristics of the three benchmark groups at age 16 in the NLSY (top panel) and in tenth grade in the ELS (bottom panel). Although it might seem intuitive to think that along most measures, GED holders would fall between dropouts and graduates (as if they were an average of the two), that is often not the case. Among the family measures, dropouts and GED holders come from slightly larger families, with 2.7 and 2.8 siblings compared with 2.3 for high school graduates. GED holders, however, are more likely to be first in the birth order (25 percent) compared with dropouts (16 percent) or graduates (22 percent) and are least likely to come from a two–biological parent family (25 percent), compared with 29 percent of dropouts and 46 percent of graduates. In addition, GED holders are more likely to have been born to a teen mother (19 percent) than dropouts (16 percent) or graduates (14 percent) were. A combination of being oldest in a single-parent family with a teen mother suggests that a motivation to leave school early might be to contribute to family income, but sample means cannot discern a causal effect, though it is important to note how the background of GED holders, motivated enough to attain a high school equivalent, differ from those of their dropout counterparts.

Where GED holders and dropouts are similar, and similarly different from high school graduates, is in measures of risk. Forty-five percent of dropouts had a mother who did not finish high school, and 44 percent had a father who did not finish high school, compared with 32 percent and 36 percent for GED holders and 26 percent and 27 percent for graduates, respectively. These shares are higher than in the CPS—but recall that the CPS conditioned on having a parent in the household, excluding 15 percent of mothers and 40 percent of fathers. The NLSY also compiles a family/home risk score and physical environment risk score (a subset of the family/home score) to capture the multiple pathways, such as lack of material resources or characteristics of the neighborhood, that could affect a child or adolescent. The

Table 3.5
Means of Family Characteristics of Dropouts, GED Holders, and High School Graduates Who Do Not Enroll in College at Age 16 (NLSY) and Grade 10 (ELS)

Family Characteristic	Dropout	GED Holder	High School Graduate
Age 16 (NLSY)			
Number of siblings	2.7	2.8	2.3
First in birth order	16%	25%	22%
Two–biological parent family	29%	25%	46%
Biological-parent/ stepparent family	19%	17%	16%
Single-parent family	38%	41%	31%
Adopted	4%	4%	3%
Lives with grandparents	2%	4%	2%
Mother was teen at child's birth	16%	19%	14%
Mother was high school dropout	45%	32%	26%
Father was high school dropout	44%	36%	27%
Family/home risk score[a]	4.1	3.7	3.2
Physical environment risk score[a]	2.0	1.8	1.5
Gun violence witness	20%	18%	12%
Deceased primary family member[b]	4%	5%	4%
Grade 10 (ELS)			
Number of siblings at home	1.7	1.4	1.5
Two–biological parent family	37%	40%	51%
Biological-parent/ stepparent family	26%	26%	22%

Table 3.5—Continued

Family Characteristic	Dropout	GED Holder	High School Graduate
Single-parent family	32%	30%	24%
Other parent situation	5%	5%	3%
Father was a high school dropout	35%	21%	18%
Mother was a high school dropout	37%	17%	17%

NOTE: Members of the 1997 NLSY sample reached age 16 in the 1997–2001 waves, depending on age at sample start. Sample is weighted using the panel weights. The ELS 2002 is a sample of tenth-graders; means are weighted with base-year student weight.

[a] Family/home risk score is based on Caldwell and Bradley (1984) *Home Observation for Measurement of the Environment* and ranges from 0 to 21. Physical environment risk score is a subset of family/home and ranges from 0 to 7. For both, a higher index indicates higher risk.

[b] A *deceased primary family member* indicates a parent or sibling has died. Benchmark groups are statistically different from the overall NLSY sample.

scores are compiled from questions answered by the respondent or the respondent's parents or from the interviewer's observations. They cover hardship and safety, such as whether the home regularly had utilities; whether it was well maintained or the neighborhood in general had well-maintained homes; family activities, such as whether the children regularly eat dinner with their parents or attend church; and parental support and involvement, such as attending a parent-teacher conference. The family/home score is out of 21 points possible, with higher score associated with more risk. The physical environment risk score is out of 7 points possible and counts only the environmental and neighborhood questions included in family/home risk, such as the frequency of hearing gunshots in the neighborhood.

The family/home and environmental risk scores are very informative about the cumulative hardships that different young adults face. The family/home risk score among dropouts was 4.1, and that for GED holders was 3.7, compared with 3.2 for graduates. Note that a family/home risk score of 4.0 is the 75th percentile of all scores, meaning that 75 percent of all respondents had lower family/home risk scores than dropouts. The environmental risk score was similar, in that dropouts and GED holders were similar (2.0 and 1.8) and higher than graduates (1.5). Dropouts and GED holders live in some combination of bad neighborhoods, low-quality housing, and family financial fragility, with less involved or less supportive parents.

In a way that can encapsulate the external risks and hardships among the three groups, the NLSY asks, in a separate part of the survey from the risk score measures, whether the respondent has ever seen someone shot or shot at, a more extreme measure than hearing gunshots in their neighborhood. One in five dropouts and GED holders responded yes, compared with 12 percent of graduates. Given that these means are taken at age 16, those rates should be interpreted to mean that one in five dropouts had seen someone get shot at by the time they were 16. The survey also asks whether the respondent has lost a family member—either a mother, father, brother, or sister. Four percent of dropouts and 5 percent of GED holders have a deceased primary family member, compared with 4 percent of graduates.

The family characteristics in the ELS are similar to those in the NLSY. The three groups have a similar number of siblings (1.7, 1.4, and 1.5). Graduates are more likely to come from two–biological parent families (51 percent) than GED holders (40 percent) or dropouts (37 percent). Dropouts are also more likely to have a father or mother who was also a high school dropout (35 percent and 37 percent) than GED holders (21 percent and 17 percent) or graduates (18 percent and 17 percent). These rates of two-parent households and parent dropouts are similar to the NLSY rates for graduates but differ among GED holders and dropouts, which could be attributed to the different samples for those two groups or to the difficulty in getting consistent estimates for small shares of the population.

The family/environment measures capture characteristics or features outside the individual's control. The individual measures, which we discuss in this section, mostly capture the youths' choices and behavior and outcomes. Again, it is not necessarily that GED holders represent an average between dropouts and graduates. Table 3.6 shows the benchmark groups at age 16 in the NLSY. By age 16, GED holders were the most likely to report sexual activity (52 percent), drinking

Table 3.6
Means of Individual Characteristics of Dropouts, GED Holders, and High School Graduates Who Do Not Enroll in College at Age 16 (NLSY)

Characteristic	Dropout	GED Holder	High School Graduate
Reported previous sexual activity	46%	52%	30%
Reported drinking alcohol	54%	61%	51%
Reported smoking marijuana	36%	42%	27%
Emotional disorder[a]	7%	6%	3%
Learning disorder	9%	6%	7%
Body mass index (BMI)	23.8	23.5	24.0
Underweight	8%	11%	11%
Overweight	20%	16%	18%
Obese	9%	10%	11%

NOTE: Members of the 1997 NLSY sample reached age 16 in the 1997–2001 waves, depending on age at sample start. Sample is weighted using the panel weights.

[a] Emotional disorders encompass eating disorders; more information can be found in Appendix 9 of the NLSY codebook (National Longitudinal Surveys, undated).

alcohol (61 percent), and smoking marijuana (42 percent), all three rates higher than for dropouts (46 percent, 54 percent, and 36 percent, respectively) and for graduates (30 percent, 51 percent, and 27 percent, respectively). Dropouts and GED holders were also more likely to have an emotional disorder, at 7 percent and 6 percent, compared with 3 percent for graduates. But dropouts were more likely to have learning disorder, at 9 percent, compared with 6 percent and 7 percent of GED holders and graduates. Hence, in addition to more family and environmental risk, dropouts have more individual behavioral challenges than GED holders and dropouts.

For BMI, the three groups do not differ, though 11 percent of GED holders are underweight, and graduates are more likely to be overweight (18 percent) or obese (11 percent) compared with GED holders and dropouts. This could reflect food insecurity among the first two groups.

Academic

Finally, we show a set of academic measures in Table 3.7, again at age 16 and grade 10 from the NLSY and ELS. The NLSY has a limited set of academic measures. The Armed Services Vocational Aptitude Battery (ASVAB) is the entrance exam for the armed services. The NLSY sample was administered the ASVAB, and members' scores were reported directly, as well as their percentile rank among three-

Table 3.7
Means of Academic Characteristics of Dropouts, GED Holders, and High School Graduates Who Do Not Enroll in College at Age 16 (NLSY) and Grade 10 (ELS)

Academic Characteristic	Dropout	GED Holder	High School Graduate
Age 16 (NLSY)			
ASVAB percentile[a]	22	34	34
Repeated a grade	50%	45%	25%
Suspended	62%	65%	41%
Grade 10 (ELS)			
Involved in high school extracurricular	27%	32%	40%
On a high school sports team	32%	33%	47%
Math quartile[b] (1 = low)	1.5	2.0	2.2
Reading quartile[b]	1.6	2.1	2.1
Lowest quartile of math and reading	48%	25%	25%
Repeated a grade K–10	43%	30%	18%
Has an IEP[c]	32%	13%	22%

Table 3.7—Continued   month age groups. Dropouts scored poorly on

Academic Characteristic	Dropout	GED Holder	High School Graduate
Number of academic risk factors[d]	2.1	1.8	1.2
No risk factors	5%	13%	24%
2–3 risk factors	29%	33%	21%
5–6 risk factors	11%	7%	4%
Dropout prevention program	7%	5%	4%
Remedial math or English class	14%	14%	13%
Special education	14%	8%	11%
Off-site vocational classes/ program	10%	10%	8%
Career academy	10%	10%	10%
Skipped a class[e]	58%	57%	34%
Absent for seven or more days[e]	37%	39%	18%
In-school suspension[e]	38%	33%	16%
Out-of-school suspension[e]	25%	24%	11%
Transferred for disciplinary reasons	7%	3%	1%

NOTE: Members of the 1997 NLSY sample reached age 16 in the 1997–2001 waves, depending on age at sample start. Sample is weighted using the panel weights. The ELS 2002 is a sample of tenth-graders; means are weighted with base-year student weight.

[a] ASVAB percentile is based on three-month age groups, discussed in Appendix 10 of the NLSY codebook (National Longitudinal Surveys, undated). Benchmark groups are statistically different from the overall NLSY sample.

[b] The ELS survey instrument includes math and reading tests (see section 2.2.2 of NCES, undated); the quartile score divides the weighted achievement distribution into four equal groups.

[c] An IEP is required by federal law for any student with a disability.

[d] There are six possible academic risk factors: single-parent household, both parents lack a high school diploma, a sibling has dropped out, two or more school changes, repeated at least one grade, and comes from a household with income under the poverty level.

[e] The time frame for behavioral questions (skipped a class, absences, in-school and out-of-school suspensions) was the previous semester. Benchmark groups are statistically different from overall ELS sample.

the ASVAB, averaging in the 22nd percentile (i.e., had a lower score than 78 percent of similar-aged respondents), but GED holders and graduates both averaged in the 34th percentile. The reverse is true for the measures of behavior in the school (academic) setting. Half of all dropouts and 45 percent of GED holders repeated a grade, and 62 percent of dropouts and 65 percent of GED holders had been suspended, compared with 25-percent grade repeaters and 41-percent suspended among graduates. This suggests that GED holders are similar in aptitude to graduates but similar in problematic behavior to dropouts, perhaps owing to the similar risks and hardship noted previously.

The ELS, being a school-based survey instead of a household survey, has many more measures of the school environment and academic aptitude and performance. To start, dropouts and GED holders participate less in school activities. Twenty-seven percent of dropouts are involved in an extracurricular activity, compared with 32 percent of GED holders and 40 percent of graduates, and 32 percent of dropouts and 33 percent of GED holders are on sports teams, compared with 47 percent of graduates.

On scholastic tests, GED holders look much more similar to graduates than to dropouts. The average math quartile (1 is the lowest) of dropouts is 1.5, while for GED holders it is 2.0 and for graduates 2.2. Similarly, for reading quartiles, dropouts average 1.6, but GED holders average 2.1 and graduates 2.1. Nearly half of dropouts are in the lowest quartile for both math and reading (48 percent), while an equal share of GED holders and graduates (25 percent) are in both. However, academically, GED holders fall behind graduates. Only 18 percent of graduates repeated a grade between kindergarten and tenth grade, compared with 30 percent of GED holders and 43 percent of dropouts. Interestingly, GED holders have lower rates of IEPs than graduates or dropouts. This could reflect school quality or success in identifying students at need, as well as the student's need for an IEP. The NLSY found that learning disability rates were lower among GED holders than the graduates or dropouts.

The ELS summarizes the family/neighborhood characteristics through a measure of *academic risk factors*. There are six possible academic risk factors: living in a single-parent household, both parents lacking high school diplomas, a sibling having dropped out, having made two or more school changes, having repeated at least one grade, and coming from a household with income under the poverty level. The average number of risk factors is 2.1 for dropouts, 1.8 for GED holders, and 1.2 for graduates. In addition, just under a quarter of graduates (24 percent) have no risk factors, compared with 13 percent of GED holders and 5 percent of dropouts, while 11 percent of dropouts have nearly every risk factor, compared with 7 percent of GED holders and 4 percent of graduates. This distribution of risk in family background is similar in the NLSY.

There is evidence from the ELS of predropout interventions. Seven percent of dropouts had participated in a dropout prevention program by tenth grade, compared with 5 percent of GED holders and 4 percent of graduates. All three groups were similarly likely to have taken a remedial class (14 percent, 14 percent, and 13 percent), but dropouts were more likely to have been in special education (14 percent) compared with 8 percent of GED holders and 11 percent of graduates. In addition, the three groups have near even rates of enrollment in off-site vocational classes and career academies.

Finally, the ELS has evidence of behavioral issues in the school setting across an array of measures. For nearly all measures, dropouts and GED holders are very similar to each other and different from graduates. Asked about the previous semester, 58 percent of dropouts and 57 percent of GED holders had skipped a class, compared with 34 percent of graduates; and 38 percent of dropouts and 39 percent of GED holders were absent for seven or more days, compared with 18 percent of graduates. Dropouts and GED holders were also much more likely to be suspended, whether in or out of school, at 38 percent in school and 25 percent out of school for dropouts, 33 percent in school and 24 percent out of school for GED holders, and only 16 percent in school and 11 percent out of school for graduates. There are numerous reasons for suspensions, and to understand the extent or severity of behavior, we also compare the share of students transferred for disciplinary reasons, which is 7 percent for dropouts, 3 percent for GED holders, and 1 percent for graduates. This suggests that the disciplinary problems among dropouts, although occurring at similar rates to those of GED holders, are more severe.

Conclusions

The aim of this chapter is to understand how dropouts, GED holders, and high school graduates who do not go on to postsecondary education differ from each other before, and as, they make their educational decisions. Understanding the differences in background and aptitude can help programs that work with the dropout population understand the challenges youths face. The literature has identified several correlates with not completing high school; we leverage three large public datasets to present those correlates numerically.

We find evidence that high school dropouts and GED holders are more likely to come from risky home and neighborhood situations than the survey populations—their parents have higher dropout rates, their mothers are more likely to be a teen parent, their homes are less well maintained and their neighborhoods more dangerous. Behaviorally, the two groups have similar disciplinary records, though there is evidence to suggest that dropouts' actions may be more severe and GED holders' more personally risky (e.g., sexual activity and drug use). But GED holders have a similar aptitude and scholastic ability to graduates, outscoring dropouts on both the ASVAB and a math and reading comprehension exam.

We take as a conclusion—and a lesson for programs like ChalleNGe—that the commonality among individuals who may enroll in the program (i.e., did not finish high school) is a very risky home environment that presents more challenges and barriers than the average student faces. Programs cannot, on the other hand, assume that those individuals are necessarily remedial or have poor academic skills; more than likely, the aptitude of dropouts will vary greatly, given that it is not possible to draw conclusions about the causes of dropping out of high school or attaining an equivalent credential instead of graduating with a diploma, in a study of sample means. A successful program will likely have to be flexible in its academic component to take varying aptitude into account.

In addition, the above means are helpful for programs like ChalleNGe in characterizing their own participant populations and forming postprogram outcome expectations. For example, around 60 percent of dropouts have been suspended, according to the NLSY—but a ChalleNGe site can have an enrolling class in which a much higher share has been suspended (the ChalleNGe RCT found much higher rates) and can conclude that its program participants have greater behavioral problems than the average dropout. Or, according to the ELS, around 14 percent of dropouts had taken a remedial math or English class; a site in which a higher share has taken remedial classes can note that its participants have more learning difficulties than the average dropout.

CHAPTER FOUR

Benchmarks of Short- and Long-Term Outcomes

In this chapter, we compare the three benchmark groups—high school dropouts, GED holders, and high school graduates—in the years after normal high school age. This can be thought of as a postintervention comparison. Again, we organize our discussion around the findings from the literature in Chapter One: education (credentials and training), employment, and health and well-being; we add civics to our analysis because it is of particular interest to ChalleNGe and the eight core components. Our aim is to add interpretable, numeric references to the general findings of the literature about the long-term outcomes associated with not finishing regular high school, for the benefit of ChalleNGe directors.

Status the Year After Leaving School

In the remainder of this chapter, we discuss outcomes of the three benchmark groups after age 19 across an array of measures. We begin by discussing the immediate status of dropouts in the year after leaving high school to establish a baseline, or starting point, for intervention programs like ChalleNGe.

To determine status, we use the CPS. As discussed in Chapter Two, the individuals in the education supplement are interviewed in two consecutive Octobers. We define *high school dropout* as an individual who was enrolled in high school in the first October but not enrolled and without a diploma or equivalent credential in the second October. Here, we summarize the enrollment and employment status of dropouts in that second October, which is sometime in the year after leaving high school. We show the result for all dropouts, and then by grade of dropping out, in Table 4.1.

In the year after leaving school, dropouts' enrollment in vocational training is low, averaging 4 percent; around 40 percent are employed, 16 percent unemployed, and nearly half (45 percent) are not in the labor force, meaning that they are neither working nor looking for work. These numbers reflect status at the time of the survey—an individual could have worked or enrolled earlier in the year. The share enrolled in vocational training does not vary much by the grade of dropping out, but employment outcomes vary directly. Only 23 per-

Table 4.1
Means of Near-Term Outcomes of Dropouts in the Year After Leaving School, by Final Grade Attended (CPS)

Outcome	All High School Dropouts (%)	9th Grade (%)	10th Grade (%)	11th Grade (%)	12th Grade (%)
Enrolled in vocational school	4	4	4	3	4
Employed	40	23[a]	30[a]	43[a]	50[a]
Full-time[b]	49	56	38	43	56
Paid hourly	91	81	94	88	96
Variable hours[c]	14	21	11	16	11
Unemployed	16	10[a]	15[a]	16[a]	18[a]
Not in the labor force	45	67[a]	55[a]	41[a]	33[a]

SOURCE: Data are from the 1996–2016 October supplements of the CPS; supplement weights were used.
NOTE: Dropouts in the CPS are identified by indicating in the initial October survey that they were enrolled and, in the second survey, 12 months later, that they were not enrolled and had not received a diploma.

[a] In the first column, dropout population is statistically different from nondropout population; in the second through fifth columns, dropout population statistically differs by year of dropout.

[b] Full-time workers are those who usually work 35 hours or more each week at their main job.

[c] Variable hours is a dummy indicating that the respondent's job does not have the same number of hours week to week.

cent of individuals who left school during ninth grade are employed a year later, while 67 percent are out of the labor force. With each additional grade, school leavers are more likely to be working and less likely to be out of the labor force. Half (50 percent) of individuals who left during twelfth grade are working, and 33 percent are out of the labor force.

Moreover, if employed, just under half of dropouts are working full time in the year after they left school (49 percent), nearly all (91 percent) are paid hourly, and 14 percent have variable hours that are not consistent week to week. Together, this suggests that the jobs are likely not career jobs. Notably, unlike job holding, these job features do not have a clear pattern with grade at leaving school. The unemployment rate increases with year of dropping out, from 10 percent to 18 percent. Unemployment is a worse outcome than employment. However, it is a better outcome than being out of the labor force. Even though unemployment means that the individual does not have a job, it indicates that they are engaged with the economy and searching for work.

Hence, immediately after leaving school (which corresponds roughly to ages 15 to 19), few high school dropouts are pursuing vocational training, a larger share are employed or looking for work but likely working part time in hourly jobs, and nearly half are not in the labor force at all. The means in Table 4.1 can be considered a starting point for intervention programs that, like ChalleNGe, have the twin goals of getting young dropouts more education and training in the near term and, in the long term, better, career-oriented jobs.

Credentials and Training

The goal of many dropout or at-risk youth intervention programs is education: for participants to attain a high school equivalency credential or to recover credit to reenroll in high school. According to the NLSY and ELS, just over half of individuals who drop out of school attain a high school equivalency credential. The rate of attainment is not constant over age. Table 4.2 shows the percentage of high school dropouts who

Table 4.2
Percentage of Dropouts with a GED, by Age (NLSY)

	Age														
	15	16	17	18	19	20	21	22	23	24	25	26	27	28	29
GED	0	2	10	18	28	34	40	45	48	51	52	54	56	58	62

SOURCE: Data are from the 1997–2015 waves of the NLSY.
NOTE: Table shows the share, at each age, of individuals who do not receive a high school diploma who had a GED. Sample is weighted using the panel weights.

have a GED at each age from 15 to 29. The share is cumulative—at age 29, for example, 62 percent of dropouts have earned a GED, either at age 29 or at a younger age. Of particular note for the Youth ChalleNGe program is that fewer than one in five high school dropouts has a high school equivalent by age 18, the age at which most traditional students finish high school and the oldest age at which individuals may enter Youth ChalleNGe. High GED attainment among cadets is an improvement on expected GED attainment by that age.

Unlike Table 4.2, which shows the cumulative attainment of the GED, Figure 4.1 shows the rate of attainment *at each age*. For each age, the numerator is the number earning a GED credential at that age and the denominator is the total number of high school dropouts who are of that age (including previous GED attainers). GED attainment is uncommon before age 17, increases at ages 17 and 18, and peaks at age 19, when 10 percent of dropouts earn a GED. The rate of attainment by age falls after age 19.

However, a GED is not the sole or final educational or training goal of most programs or most individuals. Individuals with (and, in some rare cases, without) a high school equivalent may enroll in two-year or four-year colleges. Table 4.3 shows the share of all GED holders who are enrolled in postsecondary education, by age from 19 to 29, for both two-year and four-year colleges. These do not show the share of all GED holders who have ever enrolled but the share, at any given age, who are currently enrolled. In general, enrollment in postsecondary education is low, ranging from 3 to 5 percent for two-year schools and 4 to 9 percent for four-year schools. Enrollment should not be con-

Figure 4.1
Share of High School Dropouts Earning a GED, by Age GED Awarded (NLSY, 1997 Cohort)

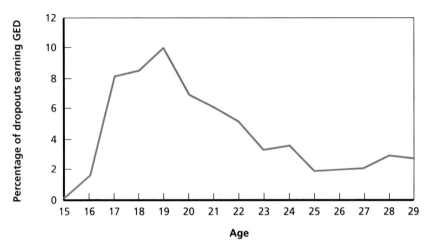

NOTES: For each age, the numerator is the number earning a GED credential, and the denominator is the total number of high school noncompleters, including those who have previously earned a GED. Age averages are based on age at the time of the survey; GED could have been awarded before prior birthday. Data are from the 1997–2015 waves of the NLSY. Sample is weighted using the panel weights.

Table 4.3
Percentage of GED Holders Who Are Enrolled in Two-Year or Four-Year Colleges, by Age (NLSY)

College	Age										
	19	20	21	22	23	24	25	26	27	28	29
Two-year	3	4	4	4	5	4	4	5	3	4	5
Four-year	4	5	6	5	6	5	6	7	5	8	9

SOURCE: Data are from the 1997–2015 waves of the NLSY.
NOTE: Table shows the share, at each age, of individuals who obtained a GED by age 29 who are enrolled in postsecondary school. Sample is weighted using the panel weights.

flated with completion. More years of school, even without a degree, are associated with higher earnings, though this is not necessarily causally related.

Outside of educational training, individuals can also pursue vocational, or occupational, training and work toward an occupational certificate. In Table 4.4, we give a range of vocational enrollment rates from ages 19 to 24 attained by our three benchmark groups: high school dropouts, GED holders, and high school graduates who did not attend college. In general, enrollment in vocational training is low, ranging from 1 to 4 percent before age 25. Dropouts have no change in enrollment between ages 19 and 24, GED holders have higher rates before age 23 and lower rates after, and graduates have the highest enrollment at age 19. Again, enrollment does not necessarily indicate graduation, certification, or completion.

In the ELS, respondents report that, by age 27, 14 percent of dropouts, 23 percent of GED holders, and 18 percent of graduates have an occupational certificate.

Employment and Earnings

Employment is key to economic stability, the primary source of income for most households, and the primary goal of many at-risk youth intervention programs. In the years immediately after youths leave school,

Table 4.4
Vocational Enrollment Rates Among Benchmark Groups, by Age (CPS)

Group	Age					
	19	20	21	22	23	24
Dropout (%)	2	2	2	2	2	2
GED holder (%)	4	3	2	4	2	1
Graduate (%)	4	3	3	1	2	2

SOURCE: Data are from the 1996–2016 October supplements of the CPS; supplement weights were used. Individuals are counted as enrolled in vocational training if they indicated in the October supplement that they were currently enrolled at the time of survey.

the biggest employment challenge for this population is the low rates of labor force participation. A large share of youths from all three of our benchmark groups, but in particular those without a high school diploma, have very low rates of working (employment) or actively looking for work (unemployment). Table 4.5 shows the range of the share of the benchmark groups who are not in the labor force at ages 19 to 24 in the CPS. High school dropouts have high rates of nonparticipation in the labor force in the first six years after the normal age of leaving high school. At 19, 36 percent of dropouts are not in the labor force, and, by age 24, this nudges slightly lower to 33 percent. As we noted in the previous section, enrollment in two-year, four-year, and vocational school is not high among dropouts and, therefore, could not account for such high rates. Conversely, graduates have a steady rate of nonparticipation over this age period, between 19 and 20 percent. GED holders, on the other hand, start with a nonparticipation rate of 27 percent at age 19 and fall to 20 percent—on par with graduates—by age 24.

For intervention programs, the means in Table 4.5 have two implications. First, one avenue for success among programs, less often noted, is increasing labor force participation by connecting youths to jobs *or* job searches. Programs that can increase sustained job search among participants after the program reduce nonparticipation in the labor force. Second, a successful program (which we define by the

Table 4.5
Labor Force Nonparticipation Rates Among Benchmark Groups, by Age (CPS)

Group	Age					
	19	20	21	22	23	24
Dropout (%)	36	37	33	32	32	33
GED holder (%)	27	25	24	24	24	20
Graduate (%)	19	20	20	20	20	20

SOURCE: Data are from the 1996–2016 October supplements of the CPS; supplement weights were used.
NOTE: An individual was counted as participating in the labor force if they indicated in the October supplement that they were currently employed or actively looking for work at the time of the survey.

status of high school graduates) may still leave one in five participants disconnected from the labor force; success is improving on the expectation (which we define by the status of high school dropouts) of 32 to 37 percent of youths out of the labor force.

The CPS's measure of labor force nonparticipation is based on status at the time of survey. Table 4.6 compares the share of youths in the NLSY who reported that they did not have a job in the prior year, by age, for each of the benchmark groups. This is not the same as participation, because it does not measure the share who were looking for a job. However, it is likely that if an individual did not have a job for a year, they either were not searching or stopped searching. Hence, the share without a job in the prior year is a similarly useful measure of labor market attachment. The rates between the CPS status and the NLSY retrospective cohere. At age 19, 38 percent of dropouts did not hold a job in the year prior, compared with 28 percent of GED holders and 19 percent of graduates. Although all groups show increase in work in their mid-20s, the rates of nonworking again return to similar levels by age 29.

We next examine the means of the benchmark groups in a range of job characteristics, conditional on the individual working. Table 4.7 shows the share of individuals who are working and then the share of workers who are full time, who are paid hourly, the share who were in the service sector, and the share who are in food service (a subset of the

Table 4.6
Share of Benchmark Groups Who Did Not Have a Job in the Prior Year, by Age (NLSY)

Group	19	20	21	22	23	24	25	26	27	28	29
Dropout (%)	38	36	37	34	33	30	32	32	35	38	39
GED holder (%)	28	22	24	24	21	20	21	23	26	23	27
Graduate (%)	19	17	13	14	14	13	15	17	17	19	21

SOURCE: Data are from the 1997–2015 waves of the NLSY.
NOTE: Sample is weighted using the panel weights. Individuals are asked to report whether they received any earned income in the calendar year prior; we define *Job in the Prior Year* by whether the respondent reported a positive income amount.

Table 4.7
Share of Individuals Employed and Job Characteristics of Employed Workers in Benchmark Groups, by Age (CPS)

Worker Characteristic	19	20	21	22	23	24
Share employed (%)						
Dropout	45	49	53	57	58	53
GED holder	60	56	64	63	65	71
Graduate	65	68	68	71	73	73
Conditional on being employed						
Share full time (%)						
Dropout	63	63	68	71	72	69
GED holder	56	61	67	70	71	79
Graduate	59	69	71	72	77	75
Share paid hourly (%)						
Dropout	88	93	93	84	82	82
GED holder	93	89	89	89	85	83
Graduate	90	93	88	88	86	88
Share in the service sector (%)						
Dropout	44	45	41	40	40	34
GED holder	44	43	34	32	38	31
Graduate	44	37	35	37	31	32
Share in food service (%)						
Dropout	20	16	17	14	15	12
GED holder	16	13	11	13	12	11
Graduate	16	12	11	11	9	10

SOURCE: Data are from the 1996–2016 October supplements of the CPS; supplement weights were used.
NOTE: *Full time* is defined as working more than 35 hours per week. The service sector comprises CPS-defined categories of occupations: food preparation and service; building and grounds cleaning and maintenance; personal care and service; and sales and related. *Food service* indicates those in food preparation and service only.

overall service sector). To start, at age 19, 45 percent of dropouts are working, compared with 60 percent of GED holders and 65 percent of graduates. These rates increase by age 24 to 53 percent for dropouts and 71 and 73 percent for GED holders and graduates. The trend over that age period is for increases in employment, but while GED holders "catch up" to graduates in terms of employment, dropout employment is nearly 20 percentage points lower.

Conditional on working, 56 to 63 percent of 19-year-old workers from any of the benchmark groups are full time. These numbers increase to age 24, when 69 to 79 percent of workers are full time. *Full time* is defined as usually working 35 hours or more per week. Throughout these ages, the vast majority of workers are paid hourly, a number ranging from 88 to 93 percent at age 19 to 82 to 88 percent at age 24. Hourly workers are less likely to have nonwage benefits, such as retirement, health care, or leave, offered as part of the job. The difference between dropouts, GED holders, and graduates in full-time status and paid-hourly status is not large, and at some ages, GED holders are more likely to be working full time and less likely to be paid hourly than graduates.

Moreover, the three groups have similar rates of working in the service sector and one of its larger subsectors, food service. At age 19, 44 percent of dropouts, GED holders, and graduates with a job are working in the service sector; by age 24, this falls to 31 to 34 percent. Again, there is little difference across the groups. Within the service sector, 20 percent of dropouts and 16 percent of GED holders and graduates are working in food service at age 19; this falls for all three groups to 10 to 12 percent by age 24.

In Table 4.8, we show two measures of earnings, again conditional on working: the average hourly wage and the average weekly wage of each of the three groups. These are the real earnings averaged from 1996 to 2016, a period of low wage growth at the bottom of the wage distribution. Hourly wages among working high school dropouts are relatively flat over this age window, from $10.20 to $12.16. GED holders, on the other hand, see wages from $10.24 to $13.61 and high school graduates from $11.05 to $12.46. Keep in mind that the individuals from the benchmark groups participating in the labor force are

Table 4.8
Earnings of Employed Workers in Benchmark Groups, by Age (CPS)

Wage, in dollars	19	20	21	22	23	24
Hourly						
Dropout	11.12	10.35	10.20	12.16	11.89	10.90
GED holder	10.67	10.24	12.83	11.22	11.50	13.61
Graduate	11.05	11.14	11.94	11.95	12.35	12.46
Weekly						
Dropout	379	437	418	464	470	403
GED holder	364	413	480	443	490	549
Graduate	398	431	458	497	501	529

SOURCE: Data are from the 1996–2016 October supplements of the CPS.
NOTE: Amounts are adjusted to reflect real 2016 dollars. Specific variables in the
CPS are "HOURWAGE" and "EARNWEEK," and respondents were asked for only the
subset of the supplement who were also in the earner study; earner study weights
were used.

not a fixed group. New and different workers can be entering or exiting the labor force over this time period, and their human capital is not fixed because they also enroll in college or technical education. There is more dispersion in weekly wages among the groups. Considering that the share working full time increases, it is not surprising that there is more growth in weekly wages, from $379 to $403 among dropouts, $364 to $549 among GED holders, and $398 to $529 among graduates, from age 19 to age 24.

Finally, in Table 4.9, we show mean annual earned income for the benchmark groups, by age. For ease of reading the table, we show the amount in thousands. The table does not condition on working, so nonworkers (with $0 in income) are included. Lower labor force participation within a group is reflected in lower group earnings. At 19, income ranges between $5,600 for dropouts to $7,100 for GED holders and $7,300 for graduates; the amounts rise by age 29 to $19,500, $22,700, and $30,200, respectively. Given that the largest differences in hourly wages over the first six years (19–24) are slightly more than

Table 4.9
Annual Earned Income Among Benchmark Groups, in Thousands, by Age
(NLSY)

Group	19	20	21	22	23	24	25	26	27	28	29
Dropout	5.6	7.1	8.4	9.4	11.6	12.6	14.2	14.8	16.2	16.3	19.5
GED holder	7.1	8.6	10.9	13.2	13.5	16.4	19.0	19.3	19.9	20.7	22.7
Graduate	7.3	10.4	13.3	15.2	17.7	20.6	23.0	24.6	25.8	27.4	30.2

SOURCE: Data are from the 1997–2015 waves of the NLSY, adjusted using panel
weights.
NOTE: Amounts are adjusted to reflect real 2016 dollars.

$3.00 ($10.20 – $13.61), these large annual income differences speak
to the importance of getting individuals into jobs, at all, rather than
into particular types of jobs.

Wage and income data should be interpreted cautiously; wages
vary widely across the country, as does the minimum wage and cost of
living. Yet, the conditional wage data in Table 4.8 can inform ChalleNGe program directors' reasonable expectations for earnings in jobs,
and both the conditional wage in Table 4.8 and the unconditional
income in Table 4.9 can help with postprogram budgeting and planning for cadets.

Civics

Most programs, whatever element of education or job training is the
focus of their intervention, have the secondary goal of helping participants be productive members of society. Youth ChalleNGe's goal
is to "intervene in and reclaim the lives of at-risk youths to produce
program graduates with the values, skills, education and self-discipline
necessary to succeed as adults" (National Guard Youth ChalleNGe,
undated). Job Corps has the mission of teaching participants the "skills
they need to become employable and independent" (JobCorps, 2013)
while YouthBuild aims to "unleash the intelligence and positive energy
of low-income young people to rebuild their communities and their

lives" (YouthBuild, 2019). We broadly group these goals as *civics*, or being good and productive citizens.

There are a handful of ways in which civics can be measured in our surveys. For each, we rely on self-reports in the survey of bad or good behavior. Because those reports may be biased (individuals may be more likely to report or exaggerate good behavior, for example), we caution here against placing much weight on a single statistic.

In Table 4.10, we show the arrest rates, as self-reported in the NLSY, of the three benchmark groups between the ages of 19 and 29. This does not cover the share who are charged or convicted but the share who reported that they had been arrested at some point in the year prior. Arrest rates of dropouts fall from 12 percent to 6 percent; GED holders fall from 15 percent to 5 percent and graduates from 6 percent to 3 percent. The key here is that, even among high school graduates, the expected arrest rate is not zero.

Both the NLSY and the ELS measure voter participation because their samples grow into voting-eligible ages. In Table 4.11, we show the ranges of voting rates in state and local elections, separately from presidential elections, at age 21 and age 27 in the ELS. The ELS asked survey respondents whether they had voted in the most recent elections. Voter participation at age 21 is low, regardless of election, and lower among dropouts than GED holders or graduates. In the presidential election, only 18 percent of dropouts voted, compared with

Table 4.10
Self-Reported Arrest Rates Across Benchmark Groups, by Age (NLSY)

Group	19	20	21	22	23	24	25	26	27	28	29
Dropout (%)	12	10	11	12	8	5	5	8	5	8	6
GED holder (%)	15	11	11	8	9	8	7	6	4	6	5
Graduate (%)	6	5	4	5	5	5	4	3	2	3	3

SOURCE: Data are from the 1997–2015 waves of the NLSY, adjusted using panel weights.
NOTE: Survey asks whether the respondent was arrested since the most recent interview one year prior.

Table 4.11
Voter Participation Rates Among Benchmark Groups, Minimum and Maximum, by Age (ELS)

Group	21		27	
	State and Local	Presidential	State and Local	Presidential
Dropout (%)	17	18	19	32
GED holder (%)	31	31	26	45
Graduate (%)	36	38	22	39

SOURCE: Data are from the age 21 and age 27 waves of the ELS, adjusted using follow-up weights from waves 2 and 3.

31 percent of GED holders and 38 percent of graduates. By age 27, reported state and local voting remained low, at 19 to 26 percent, but presidential election voting increased to 32 percent for dropouts, 45 percent for GED holders, and 39 percent for graduates. The age 27 presidential question from the ELS refers to the 2008 presidential election, which Barack Obama won and which notably saw higher turnout among minorities—who are, as previously mentioned, overrepresented among the benchmark groups. Hence, the increase in voter participation could be limited to that particular year.

The NLSY asked about voter behavior in specific election years. Because the NLSY covers a range of cohorts, the participation rates we have are not at fixed ages but over a range of ages. We present these rates in Table 4.12. The pattern is similar—midterm elections have lower turnout than presidential, and less than half of the population reports voting; graduates vote more than dropouts; and participation in elections increases with age.

Another measure of civic participation is volunteering. Again, both the NLSY and the ELS surveyed respondents about volunteering activities. In the ELS, respondents were asked how often they regularly volunteer, and, in the NLSY, respondents were asked how many times they had volunteered in the past 12 months. In Tables 4.13 and 4.14, we show the shares of the benchmark groups who indicated that they had volunteered at all, either regularly (ELS) or in the past 12 months (NLSY). In the ELS (Table 4.13), there is little difference between

Table 4.12
Voter Participation Rates Among Benchmark Groups, Minimum and Maximum, by Election (NLSY)

Group	2004 (Ages 19–23)	2006 (Ages 21–25)	2008 (Ages 23–27)	2010 (Ages 25–29)
Dropout (%)	15	14	24	17
GED holder (%)	30	17	35	27
Graduate (%)	39	24	41	29

SOURCE: Data are from the 2004, 2006, 2008, and 2010 waves of the NLSY, adjusted using panel weights.

Table 4.13
Volunteer Rates Among Benchmark Groups, by Age (ELS)

Group	21	27
Dropout (%)	15	18
GED holder (%)	21	30
Graduate (%)	30	20

SOURCE: Data are from the age 21 and age 27 waves of the ELS, adjusted using follow-up weights from waves 2 and 3.

Table 4.14
Volunteer Rates Among Benchmark Groups, by Year and Age (NLSY)

Group	2005 (Ages 20–24)	2007 (Ages 22–26)	2011 (Ages 26–30)	2013 (Ages 28–32)
Dropout (%)	27	22	24	28
GED holder (%)	28	24	32	34
Graduate (%)	30	26	33	39

SOURCE: Data are from the 2005, 2007, 2011, and 2013 waves of the NLSY, adjusted using panel weights.

Table 4.15
Military Service Rates Among Benchmark Groups, by Age (ELS)

Group	21	27
Dropout (%)	1.0	0.3
GED holder (%)	3.1	2.5
Graduate (%)	3.8	3.7

SOURCE: Data are from the age 21 and age 27 waves of the ELS, adjusted using follow-up weights from waves 2 and 3.

ages: 15 percent to 30 percent of individuals volunteered, although, at 21, graduates had a higher rate of volunteering, and, at 27, GED holders had a higher rate of volunteering.

The NLSY (Table 4.14), which captures more time periods of volunteering, also has more variation, mostly within a band of 20 to 30 percent until later ages, when it reaches approximately 25 to 40 percent. For the total NLSY population, volunteer rates are closer to 45 percent.

Finally, in Table 4.15, we show the rates of military service (measured at that age) of the three benchmark groups. Dropouts have near-zero rates of military service, likely related to the educational or test score minimum required for entry. GED holders and graduates report service rates between 2.5 percent and 3.8 percent, with graduates at marginally higher rates.

Health and Well-Being

Individuals with lower income and lower levels of education have worse health outcomes, a finding supported by decades of health research. ChalleNGe includes a physical education component, as well as instruction on health and healthy choices as part of the life skills program. We do not have many measures of health, save BMI in the NLSY, which we use to show rates for underweight and obesity in Table 4.16.

Rates of being underweight are relatively low and fall with age. At age 19, 5 percent of dropouts, 7 percent of GED holders, and 4 percent

Table 4.16
Rates of Underweight and Obesity Across Benchmark Groups (Percentage), by Age (NLSY)

Weight by Group	19	20	21	22	23	24	25	26	27	28	29
Underweight											
Dropout	5	2	3	4	3	3	3	3	3	4	5
GED holder	7	5	5	4	4	4	3	3	3	3	4
Graduate	4	5	5	4	4	3	3	3	3	2	3
Obese											
Dropout	18	21	25	27	28	27	31	31	38	41	40
GED holder	15	19	20	23	27	26	30	31	30	34	33
Graduate	16	20	21	24	25	28	30	32	33	36	35

SOURCE: Data are from the 1997–2015 waves of the NLSY, adjusted using panel weights.
NOTE: Individuals are classified as underweight or obese using the BMI measure included in the survey.

of graduates are underweight. By age 29, these rates fall to 5 percent, 4 percent, and 3 percent, respectively. Obesity, on the other hand, grows with age, starting at 15 percent to 18 percent at age 19 and increasing to 33 percent to 37 percent by age 29. While there are some differences between the benchmark groups—dropouts have slightly higher rates of obesity—those differences are small, especially relative to the strong and shared trend. Obesity rates are rising for the total population, not just young people, but the lifetime health risk of being obese at younger ages is high. Programs that can reduce or slow the climb in obesity rates can confer major health benefits.

Aside from health, we look for other measures of well-being. In Table 4.17, we show the share of each benchmark group who reported living with their parents from ages 19 to 24 in the CPS. Living with parents is not necessarily a good or bad situation; many individuals can come from difficult family situations that are unsafe or unstable. Similarly, living with parents is not necessarily a good or bad outcome. It could be a way to save money or support enrollment in higher education,

Table 4.17
Share of Benchmark Groups Who Live with Their Parents, by Age (CPS)

Group	19	20	21	22	23	24
Dropout (%)	64	60	49	40	35	28
GED holder (%)	75	54	52	50	37	39
Graduate (%)	80	70	62	52	44	35

SOURCE: Data are from the 1996–2016 October supplements of the CPS; supplement weights were used.

a function of a parent's health and need for caregiving, or avoidance of responsibility. However, we include in this report the share living with parents as a measure of well-being because the inverse—living on one's own—often signifies financial independence. This measure is not perfect; individuals not living with their parents could still be living with other family. Yet, the trend is clear—the rate of parental coresidence falls with age. For dropouts, it falls from 64 percent to 28 percent, for GED holders from 75 percent to 39 percent, and for graduates from 80 percent to 35 percent from ages 19 to 24. Throughout, dropouts have the lowest rate of parental coresidence.

Finally, in Table 4.18, we show the rates of marriage and divorce from the NLSY. For each age, we show the share of the population married or divorced at that age; it is not an accumulating flow (i.e., share married *by* 25) but a current-age status (i.e., share married *at* 25). Both marriage and divorce rise with age. Marriage rises from 9 to 12 percent to 32 to 42 percent. Dropouts start with marginally higher marriage rates but, by the late 20s, have the lowest; graduates have the highest marriage rates throughout the 20s. Divorce rises from negligible rates of 1 percent to 3 percent at age 19 to 10 percent to 13 percent by age 29. Again, dropouts have the highest divorce rate and graduates the lowest, both consistent throughout the 20s.

Conclusions

Understanding the differences in short- and long-term outcomes can help programs that work with the dropout population account for the

Table 4.18
Rates of Marriage and Divorce Across Benchmark Groups, by Age (NLSY)

Marital Status by Group	19	20	21	22	23	24	25	26	27	28	29
Married (%)											
Dropout	10	14	16	20	21	24	26	30	30	31	32
GED holder	12	16	16	18	20	21	24	28	31	34	36
Graduate	9	14	19	24	27	30	32	35	39	41	42
Divorced (%)											
Dropout	3	3	5	6	7	7	9	9	13	14	13
GED holder	2	3	5	6	8	10	12	11	10	13	13
Graduate	1	1	1	3	4	6	7	7	7	9	10

SOURCE: Data are from the 1997–2015 waves of the NLSY, adjusted using panel weights.

challenges youths face and their own contribution to success. The literature has identified several outcomes associated with not completing high school; we leverage three large public datasets to present those outcomes numerically.

The aim of this chapter is to elucidate how dropouts, GED holders, and high school graduates who do not go on to postsecondary education differ from each other after they make their educational decisions. We start by showing the age and rates at which GEDs are attained and the credentials and training pursued afterward, finding that 62 percent of dropouts will attain a GED and that peak attainment years are ages 18 to 20.

Individuals who do not finish high school or who finish high school but do not immediately enroll in college—who comprise the benchmark groups—are not observed to have high enrollment rates in either two-year, four-year, or vocational postsecondary education. By age 29, 62 percent of dropouts will earn a GED. However, enrollment rates in two-year and four-year college remains low among GED holders (3 percent to 9 percent), and completion rates are likely lower. Among all groups, enrollment in vocational programs is low at any given time, but—perhaps because they are often shorter programs— occupational credential rates are higher. By age 27, more than one in five GED holders has an occupational certificate.

The benchmark groups have low rates of labor force participation, meaning that a large share of individuals neither work nor look for work. We measure this through current status in the CPS and summaries of the year prior in the NLSY. They both suggested similar means—that approximately 40 percent of dropouts do not work, compared with 20 percent of graduates. However, conditional on working, the features of employment, from full-time status and sector of employment to hourly wage, do not vary as much between the groups—mostly hourly work in the service sector, with pay slightly above minimum wage, and low rates of full-time work at younger ages. Hence, at least in the short term, the challenge is getting dropouts and GED holders into jobs.

The difference in job holding can at least partly explain the population-level outcomes in annual income. By age 29, high school graduates are earning almost 50 percent more in a year than dropouts, according to the NLSY, but the difference in wages was less than 20 percent. These income differences emphasize how important labor force attachment and employment are to long-term successful outcomes. That is, high school graduates earn slightly higher wages than dropouts and GED holders, but the key difference is that they work much more than dropouts or GED holders. We take as a conclusion for ChalleNGe that job search is likely difficult among graduates and that discouragement or labor force dropout may be a persistent challenge.

From the measures of being "a good citizen" that we can detect, the largest difference between the groups is among arrest rates and military service. High school dropouts and GED holders are more likely to report being arrested, but the rates of all groups fall with age. And dropouts, likely because they do not meet minimum education requirements, are much less likely to serve in the military at any point. Otherwise, the groups have similar voting patterns—higher in presidential elections and increasing with age—and similar volunteering rates—roughly similar and increasing with age. They also have similar outcomes in terms of health, independent living, marriage, and divorce. Although following the same trend, dropouts are slightly more likely to divorce and less likely to marry.

CHAPTER FIVE

Benchmarks of Success

In this chapter, we distill the numerous and detailed findings presented in the previous two chapters to establish a set of population benchmarks to inform site directors developing expectations of reasonable outcomes for their program participants. The population means we present in this chapter are the central contribution of our report. Rather than establish a control group and follow the members over time, as is done in an RCT, we instead provide a population average to use as a reasonable comparison at any time. This information may be used to understand the unique needs of cadets coming into the program and upon leaving the program, to develop site-specific policy to take those needs into account, and as a rule-of-thumb reference for programs to use in measuring their own success.

Preprogram Benchmarks: Background Characteristics, Ages 14 to 16

To start, we compare the three benchmark groups—high school dropouts, GED holders, and high school graduates—around the time that dropouts leave high school. This can be thought of as a preintervention comparison. Cadets in the ChalleNGe program come from a variety of backgrounds and situations that ultimately resulted in their leaving high school (whether it was their decision or not). It can be difficult for site directors to have a reference of what is expected from young dropouts versus what is atypical, or how their cadets differ from dropouts in general.

As we discussed in Chapter One, the literature on high school dropouts identifies characteristics that correlate with not getting a high school diploma: demographic correlates, socioeconomic correlates (which we divide into family and individual characteristics), and academic correlates. When we compared the benchmark groups at ages 14 to 16 in the CPS, NLSY, and ELS, we found the following:

- **Demographic characteristics:** *All three benchmark groups were disproportionately more male and less white than high school graduates who go to college.* The share male varied little across the three groups, but dropouts and GED holders had higher shares of individuals who are black or Hispanic.

- **Family characteristics:** *Dropouts and GED holders were similar on family background correlates.* Both were more likely than graduates to come from a single-parent family, have a parent who did not finish high school, have been exposed to gun violence, and have a deceased primary family member. The NLSY has a composite measure that summarizes the risks associated with an individual's neighborhood and housing; both dropouts and GED holders came from living situations with much higher risk scores than graduates. Or, when it comes to family background, dropouts and GED holders look alike; both groups are different from graduates.

- **Individual characteristics:** *GED holders were more likely to report engaging in risky behavior outside of school than either dropouts or graduates but had similar behavior to dropouts inside school.* GED holders reported higher rates of drinking alcohol and smoking marijuana than the other two groups but had similar rates to those of dropouts of in-school and out-of-school suspension, absences, repeated grades, and skipped classes. The exception is that dropouts had much higher rates than GED holders had of being transferred for disciplinary reasons. Although there were some differences between them, dropouts and GED holders look different from graduates.

- **Academic characteristics:** *GED holders were much more similar to graduates than to dropouts in aptitude and test scores.* GED holders and graduates had similar average percentile scores on the ASVAB, which was administered to the NLSY sample, and similar quantile shares on the math and reading tests that were administered to the ELS sample. Both outperformed dropouts.

We distill the findings of Chapter Three into Table 5.1, which provides the range of the benchmark groups along key measures. This table is intended to serve as a reference for ChalleNGe site directors to gauge how site participants may differ from the average in the target population. The range covers the high and low mean values of the benchmark groups—often, though not always, set by dropouts and graduates.

We show a range that includes high school graduates, rather than a summary of dropouts only, to add context and perspective in interpreting the statistics. For example, we found in the NLSY that 20 percent of dropouts and GED holders had witnessed gun violence by the time they were 16 years old, compared with 12 percent of high school graduates. The range of 12 percent to 20 percent reflects that the difference between dropouts and nondropouts is not a cliff but a gradient. From this, a site director can conclude that at least one in ten cadets had likely been exposed to gun violence—but if more than two in ten had, then their cadets were from particularly dangerous neighborhoods or risky environments.

We also found in the ELS that 43 percent of dropouts had repeated a grade, compared with 30 percent of GED holders and 18 percent of graduates. Rather than report only the 43-percent estimate, we present the range of 18 percent to 43 percent, which reflects that the difference between dropouts and nondropouts is a gradient and that there is wide variation, even among the target population, in this particular measure of academic risk. Again, a site director can conclude that, if their cadets have higher rates of repeating a grade (say, more than half have repeated), then their participants have struggled in the academic setting more than expected—but, at the very least, likely one in five cadets has repeated a grade.

Table 5.1
Range of Characteristics of Benchmark Groups, Ages 14 to 16

Characteristic	Range	Table in Report	Data Source(s)
Demographic and family			
Male	55–61%	3.1 column 1; 3.2	CPS, NLSY, ELS
White (non-Hispanic)	39–68%	3.1 column 1; 3.2	CPS, NLSY, ELS
Black (non-Hispanic)	15–24%	3.1 column 1; 3.2	CPS, NLSY, ELS
Hispanic[a]	14–29%	3.1 column 1; 3.2	CPS, NLSY, ELS
Two–biological parent family	25–51%	3.5	NLSY, ELS
Single-parent family	24–41%	3.5	NLSY, ELS
Mother was high school dropout	17–45%	3.5	NLSY, ELS
Father was high school dropout	18–44%	3.5	NLSY, ELS
Deceased primary family member[b]	4–5%	3.5	NLSY
Family/home risk score[c]	3.2–4.1	3.5	NLSY
Physical environment risk score[c]	1.5–2.0	3.5	NLSY
Gun violence witness	12–20%	3.5	NLSY
Individual			
Reported previous sexual activity	30–52%	3.6	NLSY
Reported drinking alcohol	51–61%	3.6	NLSY
Reported smoking marijuana	27–42%	3.6	NLSY
Emotional disorder[d]	3–7%	3.6	NLSY
Learning disorder	6–9%	3.6	NLSY
Underweight	8–11%	3.6	NLSY
Overweight	16–20%	3.6	NLSY
Obese	9–11%	3.6	NLSY
Academic			
ASVAB percentile (1 = low)[e]	22–34	3.7	NLSY
Repeated a grade	18–50%	3.7	NLSY, ELS

Table 5.1—Continued

Characteristic	Range	Table in Report	Data Source(s)
Lowest quartile of math and reading[f]	25–48%	3.7	ELS
Has an IEP[g]	13–32%	3.7	ELS
In-school dropout prevention program	4–7%	3.7	ELS
Remedial math or English class	13–14%	3.7	ELS
In-school suspension	16–38%	3.7	ELS
Out-of-school suspension	11–25%	3.7	ELS

NOTE: This table presents, for each variable listed, the range of sample averages of dropouts, GED holders, and graduates in the survey listed in the rightmost column. Multiple surveys listed indicates the variable was found in multiple surveys, and the range spans the sample averages of all three surveys. For the CPS, data are from the 1996–2016 October supplements of the CPS; supplement weights were used. Dropouts in the CPS are identified by indicating in the initial October survey that they were enrolled and, in the second survey, 12 months later, that they were not enrolled and had not received a diploma. For the NLSY, members of the 1997 NLSY sample reached age 16 in the 1997–2001 waves, depending on age at sample start. The sample is weighted using the panel weights. For the ELS, the ELS 2002 is a sample of tenth-graders; means are weighted with base-year student weight.

[a] Hispanic and white (or black) are not exclusive categories, because white or black is race and Hispanic is ethnicity. We define Hispanic as an ethnic group and remove from the black and white race categories anyone of Hispanic ethnicity, to make the categories mutually exclusive.

[b] A *deceased primary family member* indicates a parent or sibling has died.

[c] Family/home risk score is based on Caldwell & Bradley (1984) and ranges from 0 to 21. Physical environment risk score is a subset of Family/home and ranges from 0 to 7. For both, a higher index indicates higher risk.

[d] Emotional disorders encompass eating disorders; more information can be found in Appendix 9 of the NLSY codebook (National Longitudinal Surveys, undated).

[e] ASVAB percentile is based on three-month age groups, discussed in Appendix 10 of the NLSY codebook (National Longitudinal Surveys, undated). Benchmark groups are statistically different from the overall NLSY sample.

[f] The ELS survey instrument includes math and reading tests (see section 2.2.2 of NCES, undated); the quartile score divides the weighted achievement distribution into four equal groups.

[g] An IEP is required by federal law for any student with a disability.

In this way, these ranges can help inform directors of how a cadet compares to the spectrum-of-selection population to identify the unique needs of their program participants.

Postprogram Benchmarks: Immediate Outcomes, Ages 17 to 19

The age range for the ChalleNGe program is 16 to 18, aligning ChalleNGe's intervention with the time of or immediately after leaving school. Sites track cadets' placement for one year after the end of the Residential Phase. Although any one site can compare one cohort with another, it can be difficult for directors to know how their placement outcomes compare to where cadets would have been in the absence of ChalleNGe or what is successful versus not. We thus compared outcomes of the benchmark groups at ages 17 to 19 in the CPS, NLSY, and ELS. We found the following:

- *Over half of dropouts obtained a GED by their late 20s, but the most common ages of attainment are 17 to 20 years old.* Cadets who attain a GED during ChalleNGe, when they are 16 to 18, are earlier-than-average GED earners.
- *Enrollment in vocational school is low among dropouts and GED holders.* Although a larger share of individuals in the benchmark groups earned an occupational certificate by their late 20s, enrollment at any given time is low, particularly at younger ages.
- *A large share of recent dropouts was out of the labor force, neither working nor looking for work.* The share out of the labor force decreases with age, and the share employed increases with age, but there is still a large number of dropouts and GED holders who are nonparticipants. However, even among graduates, labor force participation rates and employment rates were low at 17 to 19 years old.

We distill these findings and others from Chapter Three into Table 5.2. This table is intended to serve as a reference for site directors

Table 5.2
Range of Characteristics of Benchmark Groups, Ages 17 to 19

Characteristic	Dropouts and GED Holders Only, 17 and 18 Years Old (%)	All Benchmark Groups, 19 Years Old	Table in Report	Data Source
GED attainment	10–18	28%[a]	4.2	NLSY
Enrolled in vocational school	3–4	2–4%	4.1, 4.4	CPS
Employed	30–43	45–65%	4.1, 4.7	CPS
Full time[b]	38–43	56–63%	4.1, 4.7	CPS
Paid hourly	88–94	88–93%	4.1, 4.7	CPS
In the service sector[c,d]		44%	4.7	CPS
In food service[c,d]		16–20%	4.7	CPS
Hourly wage[c]		$10.67–$11.12	4.8	CPS
Not in the labor force	41–55	19–36%	4.1, 4.5	CPS
Lives with parents[c]		64–80%	4.17	CPS
Self-reported arrest[e]		6–15%	4.10	NLSY
Underweight[f]		4–7%	4.16	NLSY
Obese[f]		15–18%	4.16	NLSY

NOTE: This table presents, for each variable listed, the range of sample averages of dropouts, GED holders, and graduates in the survey listed in the rightmost column. For the NLSY, data are from the 1997–2015 waves of the NLSY. Sample is weighted using the panel weights. For the CPS, data are from the 1996–2016 October supplements; supplement weights were used. Dropouts in the CPS are identified by indicating in the initial October survey that they were enrolled and, in the second survey, 12 months later, that they were not enrolled and had not received a diploma. We assume that 17- and 18-year-olds correspond to tenth- and eleventh-grade school leavers. Hourly wages are adjusted to real 2016 dollars.

[a] This estimate includes dropouts only and describes GED attainment by age 19.

[b] Full-time workers are those who usually work 35 hours or more each week at their main job.

[c] We do not show estimates for 17 and 18 years old for certain categories because of data or definitional concerns.

Table 5.2—Continued

[d] The service sector comprises CPS-defined categories of occupations: food preparation and service; building and grounds cleaning and maintenance; personal care and service; sales and related. *Food service* means those in food preparation and service only.

[e] Self-reported arrest covers a one-year period, defined as the 12 months prior to the most recent interview.

[f] Individuals are classified as underweight or obese using the BMI measure included in the survey.

to compare their own site's placement statistics with target population averages at similar ages. In the first column, we show the baseline outcomes of dropouts and GED holders ages 17 and 18. In the second, we show the range of the benchmark groups at age 19. The reason for this is that graduates are still enrolled full-time in high school through age 18 and therefore not an appropriate comparison at that age.

Again, we show ranges at each age to add context and perspective in interpreting the statistics, as well as to not lean too heavily on a single estimate. For example, in the first column, we show that, among 17- and 18-year-olds who are not in high school, only 30 percent to 43 percent are employed. By age 19, among all three benchmark groups, 45 percent to 65 percent of individuals are employed. A site director can read this thus: On the low end, getting 30 percent of cadets placed into employment is the expected outcome of the population, without the benefit of a ChalleNGe intervention. Indeed, placing half of cadets in employment of any kind is a high bar, especially at younger ages. However, placement into employment above 65 percent, even conditional on older cadets, is likely an unreasonable goal. Similarly, if we consider employed workers, at 17 and 18, just under half are working full time (38 percent to 43 percent) and, at 19, just over half are working full time (56 percent to 63 percent). It is not the case that getting all employed cadets into full-time positions is impossible, but even high school graduates with a diploma are not working full-time at that rate.

Another example, and one that is highly telling, is the share of benchmark groups who are not in the labor force, meaning that they are neither working nor looking for work. Among 17- and 18-year-olds not in high school, this is 41 percent to 55 percent of the population. Among 19-year-olds, it is 19 percent to 36 percent. Keep in mind that enrollment in vocational school is less than 4 percent at this time and that, without a GED, most are not eligible to enroll in two- or four-year college. These rates make clear the baseline expectation on which ChalleNGe can aim to improve: getting more than half of cadets placed into *something*, even if that something is active job search. Again, we look to the 19-year-old comparison, which includes graduates, to note that nonparticipation in the labor force is still relatively high, at 19 percent to 36 percent. The baseline expectation in placing cadets is that up to half would not be in the labor force, but the reasonable cap on improving that baseline is that one in five would not be in the labor force.

The way to interpret Table 5.2 then, is this: The column examining 17- and 18-year-old dropouts is the baseline expectation of how cadets will fare after the program, rates on which ChalleNGe hopes to improve. The column examining the benchmark groups at age 19 establishes reasonable limits to those improvements. Thus, site directors should not expect that a 16-year-old cadet who finishes the residential phase will have better outcomes at 17 and 18 than a high school graduate with a diploma has at 19.

Postprogram Benchmarks: Longer-Term Outcomes, Ages 20 to 29

ChalleNGe graduates are tracked for only 12 months after finishing the program; sites do not keep count of longer-term outcomes, which we define as those achieved by age 29. However, the literature regarding high school dropouts in the long term shows that not having a high school diploma is associated with worse performance in the labor market, measured either through earnings or employment; worse physical and mental health; higher rates of arrest, substance abuse, and smoking; and higher likelihood of being on government assistance. Our key findings in comparing the benchmark groups over this period in the CPS, NLSY, and ELS are as follows:

- *A small but significant share of the benchmark groups attained an occupational or technical certificate.* We did not analyze the quality of the certificate or the labor market outcomes associated with certificates, which can vary greatly.
- *Enrollment in two-year or four-year postsecondary education was low (less than 5 percent) for GED holders.* Only a small share of GED holders was enrolled in postsecondary education at any given time, and enrollment was lowest at younger ages. Moreover, enrollment alone does not signify completion or degree attainment. Whether due to cost, difficulty of classes, or preferences for schooling, postsecondary education is not the modal pathway for GED holders, but rather the exception.
- *Labor force participation varied greatly across the benchmark groups.* We did not find large differences in the types of jobs or measurable quality of jobs in which individuals in the benchmark groups were employed. Most were hourly workers, half were in the service sector, and those employed were making similar wages. However, dropouts had much lower rates of employment (work) or unemployment (actively looking for work) than GED holders or graduates.
- *The difference in annual income between the groups started small but grew with age, likely related to labor force participation.* Income differences across the three groups increased with age. Because the earnings of employed workers were not that dissimilar, the 50-percent lower income among dropouts is likely due to 50-percent lower labor force participation rather than 50-percent lower hourly wages. This underscores the challenge of getting individuals into any job, rather than into certain types of jobs.
- *In terms of negative civic outcomes, self-reported arrest rates were highest among dropouts but were not zero among graduates. For all groups, arrests fell with age.* The rates of being arrested, as reported in the NLSY, peak at age 18 and fall over time. Even among graduates, however, there is an expectation that a small share of them had been arrested in any given year.
- *In terms of positive civic outcomes, self-reported volunteering and voting rates vary with education; dropouts vote and volunteer the*

least, and graduates vote and volunteer the most. For all groups, voting and volunteering increase with age. Voter turnout is larger in presidential elections than state and local ones, much like voter participation rates overall. Although we do not have annual measures of voting and volunteering (the former is not always a possibility), the rates captured at various ages suggest that both increase with age.

- *Military service is similar among graduates and GED holders.* Effectively 0 percent of dropouts serve in the military, likely because they do not meet the education requirements, but service among GED holders was at similar rates to those of high school graduates.

- *Among measures of well-being, there are few differences among the benchmark groups: They have similar rates of obesity, underweight, marriage, divorce, and independent living.* The benchmark groups were not identical—dropouts tended to live independently earlier, for example, and have slightly higher divorce rates—but they were close in means and trended apace.

In Table 5.3, we show the range of the benchmark groups along key measures. We divide our table into two age ranges; in the left column, we look at the range of averages between ages 20 and 24, and, in the next column, we look at the range of averages between ages 25 and 29. Given that site directors do not have data for their former cadets in this age range, these estimates are meant to help directors understand their participants' needs and challenges *after* the program ends and possibly influence a site's policy to take those challenges or needs into account.

For example, we found that, in terms of civic participation, voting among the benchmark groups had a comparable range in both age groups, 14 percent to 39 percent at ages 20 to 24 and 17 percent to 45 percent at ages 25 to 29; volunteer rates were similar, at 15 percent to 30 percent and 18 percent to 39 percent, respectively. A site director can read this thusly: The expectation for dropouts is that, at most, half will vote and a third will volunteer in their 20s, but the reality is that closer to 15 percent will do either. This is not an outcome that is

Table 5.3
Range of Outcomes of Benchmark Groups, Ages 20 to 29

Outcome	20–24 Years Old	25–29 Years Old	Table in Report	Source
Credentials and training				
Dropouts with GED[a]	34–51%	52–62%	4.2	NLSY
GED holders enrolled in college[b]	4–6%	3–9%	4.3	NLSY
Enrolled in vocational school	1–4%		4.4	CPS
Has occupational/technical certificate		14–18%	(text)	ELS
Employment and earnings				
Employed	49–73%		4.7	CPS
Full time[c]	61–79%		4.7	CPS
Paid hourly	82–93%		4.7	CPS
In the service sector[d]	31–45%		4.7	CPS
In food service[d]	9–17%		4.7	CPS
Hourly wage[e]	$10.20–$13.61		4.8	CPS
Not in the labor force	20–37%		4.5	CPS
Did not work in the prior year[e]	13–37%	15–39%	4.6	NLSY
Annual earnings (thousands)[f]	$7.1–$20.6	$14.20–30.20	4.9	NLSY
Civics				
Self-reported arrest[g]	4–12%	2–8%	4.10	NLSY
Voted	14–39%	17–45%	4.11, 4.12	ELS, NLSY
Volunteered	15–30%	18–39%	4.13, 4.14	ELS, NLSY
In military service	1–4%	0–4%	4.15	ELS
Health and well-being				
Underweight[h]	2–5%	2–5%	4.16	NLSY
Obese[h]	19–28%	29–41%	4.16	NLSY
Lives with parents	28–70%		4.17	CPS

Table 5.3—Continued

Outcome	20–24 Years Old	25–29 Years Old	Table in Report	Source
Married	14–30%	24–42%	4.18	NLSY
Divorced	1–10%	7–14%	4.18	NLSY

NOTE: This table presents, for each variable listed, the range of sample averages of dropouts, GED holders, and graduates in the survey listed in the right-hand column. Multiple surveys listed indicates the variable was found in multiple surveys, and the range spans the sample averages of all three surveys. For the NLSY, data are from the 1997–2015 waves of the NLSY. Sample is weighted using the panel weights.For the CPS, data are from the 1996–2016 October supplements; supplement weights were used. Dropouts in the CPS are identified by indicating in the initial October survey that they were enrolled and, in the second survey, 12 months later, that they were not enrolled and had not received a diploma. For the ELS, data are from the age 21 and age 27 waves of the ELS, adjusted using follow-up weights from waves 2 and 3.

[a] This is not a range of benchmarks but the share of all dropouts who have a GED.

[b] Covers two- and four-year colleges but describes exclusively GED holders.

[c] Full-time workers are those who usually work 35 hours or more each week at their main job.

[d] The service sector comprises CPS-defined categories of occupations: food preparation and service; building and grounds cleaning and maintenance; personal care and service; sales and related. *Food service* means those in food preparation and service only.

[e] Hourly wages and annual income are adjusted to real 2016 dollars.

[f] Includes individuals who did not work and earned $0.

[g] Self-reported arrest covers a one-year period, defined as the 12 months prior to the most recent interview.

[h] Individuals are classified as underweight or obese using the BMI measure included in the survey.

measured in the first year after the program but one that site directors can keep in mind as they build their core component curricula—in particular, the areas of responsible citizenship and service to community. Another example: Obesity rates among the benchmark groups climb from 19 percent to 28 percent, at ages 20 to 24, to 29 percent to 41 percent at age 25 to 29. Obesity is a serious challenge facing the target population as its members grow older, affecting over a third of individuals before they are 30. This is another example that site directors can keep in mind as they build their core component curricula—in particular, the areas of health and hygiene and physical fitness.

The postprogram outcomes can also help directors in working with cadets on their post-residential action plan. From ages 20 to 24, the average hourly wage earned, conditional on working, was $10.20 on the low end and $13.61 on the high end. By age 30, the highest annual income was $30,000. These concrete estimates of future resources can help directors advise cadets when forming their action plans. Or, the postprogram outcomes can help site directors target areas in which there is room for improvement. For example, even in their late 20s, 15 percent to 39 percent of the benchmark group members had not worked in the prior year, meaning that they likely did not participate in the labor force. Some individuals chose not to work—if, for example, they are taking care of children or enrolled full time in education—but this likely cannot explain all of the nonworkers. It is perhaps the case that many young adults with less education grow frustrated in the labor market and give up looking. Hence, program directors with an eye to long-term outcomes can think about how to incorporate not only job skills into their curricula but also job search skills.

Conclusion

The Youth ChalleNGe program is an intensive intervention in the lives of 16- to 18-year-old youths who have dropped out of high school. Programs draw participants from a portion of the population who often come from risky or difficult backgrounds who are expected to have worse outcomes in the long term. This report is intended to be used by directors to put numbers to backgrounds and outcomes with which to support their sites' program and policy development. Our aim is to not only help sites identify unique needs but also give sites reference points against which to measure their own success.

References

Allensworth, E., 2005. *Graduation and Dropout Trends in Chicago: A Look at Cohorts of Students from 1991 Through 2004*, Chicago, Ill.: Consortium on Chicago School Research.

Angrist, J., and A. Krueger, 1991. "Does Compulsory School Attendance Affect Schooling and Earnings?" *Quarterly Journal of Economics*, Vol. 106, pp. 979–1014.

Aspen Institute Forum for Community Solutions, undated. "Who Are Opportunity Youth?" webpage. As of May 20, 2020: https://aspencommunitysolutions.org/who-are-opportunity-youth/

Autor, D. H., L. F. Katz, and M. S. Kearney, 2008. "Trends in U.S. Wage Inequality: Revising the Revisionists," *Review of Economics and Statistics*, Vol. 90, No. 2, pp. 300–323.

Balfanz, R., and N. Letgers, 2004. "Locating the Dropout Crisis: Which High Schools Produce the Nation's Dropouts? Where Are They Located? Who Attends Them?" Baltimore, Md.: Center for Social Organization of Schools, Johns Hopkins University.

Berk, J., L. Rosenberg, L. Cattell, J. Lacoe, L. Fox, M. Dang, and E. Brown, 2018. *The External Review of Job Corps: An Evidence Scan Report*, Washington, D.C.: Mathematica Policy Research report submitted to the U.S. Department of Labor.

Bloom, D., A. Gardenhire-Crooks, and C. Mandsager, 2009. *Reengaging High School Dropouts: Early Results of the National Guard Youth ChalleNGe Program Evaluation*, New York: MDRC.

Boesel, D., N. Alsalam, and T. M. Smith, 1998. *Educational and Labor Market Performance of GED Recipients*, Washington, D.C.: Office of Educational Research and Improvement, U.S. Department of Education.

Boudett, K. P., R. J. Murnane, and J. B. Willett, 2000. "Second-Chance Strategies for Women Who Drop out of School," *Monthly Labor Review*, Vol. 123, No. 12, pp. 19–31.

Bowen, N. K., and G. L. Bowen, 1999. "Effects of Crime and Violence in Neighborhoods and Schools on the School Behavior and Performance of Adolescents," *Journal of Adolescent Research*, Vol. 14, No. 3, pp. 319–342.

Brennan, Tim, and Frank Anderson, 1990. *A Longitudinal Study of Factors Producing High School Dropout: Among Handicapped and Non-Handicapped Students*, Office of Educational Research and Improvement, U.S. Department of Education.

Bridgeland, J. M., J. J. Dilulio, and R. Balfanz, 2009. *On the Front Lines of Schools: Perspectives of Teachers and Principals on the High School Dropout Problem*, Washington, D.C.: Civic Enterprises.

Bridgeland, J. M., J. J. Dilulio, and K. B. Morison, 2006. *The Silent Epidemic: Perspectives of High School Dropouts*, Washington, D.C.: Civic Enterprises.

Byrne, D., S. McCoy, and D. Watson, 2008. *The School-Leavers Survey 2007*, Dublin: Economic and Social Research Institute and Department of Education and Skills of the Government of Ireland.

Cabus, S. J., and K. De Witte, 2016. "Why Do Students Leave Education Early? Theory and Evidence on High School Dropout Rates," *Journal of Forecasting*, Vol. 35, pp. 690–702.

Caldwell, B. M., and Bradley, R. H., 1984. *Home Observation for Measurement of the Environment*, revised ed., Little Rock, Ark.: University of Arkansas.

Cameron, S. V., and J. J. Heckman, 1993. "The Nonequivalence of High School Equivalents," *Journal of Labor Economics*, Vol. 11, No. 47.

Card, D., 1999. "The Causal Effect of Education on Earnings," in O. Ashenfelter and D. Card, eds., *Handbook of Labor Economics*, Amsterdam: Elsevier, pp. 1801–1863.

Chappell, S. L., P. O'Connor, C. Withington, and D. A. Stegelin, 2015. *A Meta-Analysis of Dropout Prevention Outcomes and Strategies (A Technical Report in Collaboration with the Center for Educational Partnerships at Old Dominion University)*, Clemson, S.C.: National Dropout Prevention Center/Network at Clemson University.

Clark, M. A., and D. A. Jaeger, 2006. "Natives, the Foreign-Born and High School Equivalents: New Evidence on the Returns to the GED," *Journal of Population Economics*, Vol. 19, No. 4, pp. 769–793.

Cornell, D., A. Gregory, F. Huang, and X. Fan, 2013. "Perceived Prevalence of Teasing and Bullying Predicts High School Dropout Rates," *Journal of Educational Psychology*, Vol. 105, pp. 138–149.

Corps Network, undated. "Opportunity Youth Service Initiative," webpage. As of May 20, 2020:
https://corpsnetwork.org/our-impact/programs-initiatives/opportunity-youth-service-initiative/

Fine, Michelle, 1986. "Why Urban Adolescents Drop Into and Out of Public High School," *Teachers College Record*, Vol. 87, No. 3, pp. 393–409.

Flood, S., M. King, S. Ruggles, and J. R. Warren, 2017. *Integrated Public Use Microdata Series*, Current Population Survey, Version 5.0, dataset, Minneapolis: University of Minnesota.

Great Schools Partnership, undated. "Glossary of Education Reform," homepage. As of May 20, 2020:
https://www.edglossary.org

Grossman, M., 2006. "Education and Nonmarket Outcomes," in E. Hanushek and F. Welch, eds., *Handbook of the Economics of Education*, Amsterdam: North-Holland.

Hammond, C., D. Linton, J. Smink, and S. Drew, 2007. *Dropout Risk Factors and Exemplary Programs: A Technical Report*, Clemson, S.C.: National Dropout Prevention Center, Communities in Schools.

Heckman, J. J., J. E. Humphries, and N. S. Mader, 2010. "The GED," Cambridge, Mass., National Bureau of Economic Research Working Paper 16064.

Heckman, J. J., and P. A. LaFontaine, 2006. "Bias-Corrected Estimates of GED Returns," *Journal of Labor Economics*, Vol. 24, No. 3, pp. 661–700.

Humphries, J. E., 2010. "Young GEDs: The Growth and Change in GED Test Takers," unpublished manuscript, University of Chicago.

Institute of Education Sciences and U.S. Department of Education, 2011. "Characteristics of GED Recipients in High School: 2002–06," issue brief, U.S. Department of Education, Washington, D.C.

Issuelab by Candid, undated. "Disconnected Youth," website. As of May 20, 2020:
https://disconnectedyouth.issuelab.org/?coverage=&author=&funder=&publisher
=&wikitopic_categories=&keywords=&pubdate_start_year=1&pubdate_end_
year=1&sort=&categories=

Jepsen, C., P. Mueser, and K. Troske, 2017. "Second Chance for High School Dropouts? A Regression Discontinuity Analysis of Postsecondary Educational Returns to the GED," *Journal of Labor Economics*, Vol. 35, No. S1.

Job Corps, undated. "Job Corps Reports: Performance, Planning, and Recruitment," webpage, U.S. Department of Labor. As of May 20, 2020:
https://www.jobcorps.gov/job-corps-reports

———, 2013. "About Job Corps," obsolete webpage.

Kaufman, P., D. Bradbury, and J. Owings, 1992. "Characteristics of At-Risk Students," in *National Education Longitudinal Study of 1988*, Washington, D.C.: National Center for Education Statistics.

Kenkel, D., D. Lillard, and A. Mathios, 2006. "The Roles of High School Completion and GED Receipt in Smoking and Obesity," *Journal of Labor Economics*, Vol. 24, No. 3, pp. 635–660.

Lamote, C., S. Speybroeck, W. Van Den Noortgate, and J. van Damme, 2013. "Different Pathways Towards Dropout: The Role of Engagement in Early School Leaving," *Oxford Review of Education*, Vol. 39, pp. 739–760.

Lansford, J. E., K. A. Dodge, G. S. Pettit, and J. E. Bates, 2016. "A Public Health Perspective on School Dropout and Adult Outcomes: A Prospective Study of Risk and Protective Factors from Age 5 to 27 Years," *Journal of Adolescent Health*, Vol. 58, pp. 652–658.

Liem, J. H., K. Lustig, and C. Dillon, 2010. "Depressive Symptoms and Life Satisfaction Among Emerging Adults: A Comparison of High School Dropouts and Graduates," *Journal of Adult Development*, Vol. 17, pp. 33–43.

Mahoney, J. L., 2014. "School Extracurricular Activity Participation and Early School Dropout: A Mixed-Method Study of the Role of Peer Social Networks," *Journal of Educational and Developmental Psychology*, Vol. 4, pp. 143–154.

Maloney, T., 1991. "Estimating the Returns to a Secondary Education for Female Dropouts," discussion paper, Institute for Research on Poverty, University of Wisconsin, Madison.

Maralani, V., 2006. "From GED to College: The Role of Age and Timing in Educational Stratification," Los Angeles: California Center for Population Research, Online Working Paper Series.

———, 2011. "From GED to College: Age Trajectories of Nontraditional Educational Paths," *American Educational Research Journal*, Vol. 48, No. 5, pp. 1058–1090.

Marcotte, D. E., 2013. "High School Dropout and Teenage Childbearing," *Economics of Education Review*, Vol. 34, pp. 258–268.

Maynard, B. R., C. P. Salas-Wright, and M. G. Vaughn, 2015. "High School Dropouts in Emerging Adulthood: Substance Use, Mental Health Problems, and Crime," *Community Mental Health Journal*, Vol. 51, No. 3, pp. 289–299.

McFarland, J., J. Cui, and P. Stark, 2018. *Trends in High School Dropout and Completion Rates in the United States: 2014*, Washington, D.C.: National Center for Education Statistics.

Measure of America, Social Science Research Council, undated. "Youth Disconnection," webpage. As of May 20, 2020: http://measureofamerica.org/disconnected-youth/

Millenky, M., D. Bloom, and C. Dillon, 2010. *Making the Transition: Interim Results of the National Guard Youth ChalleNGe Evaluation*, New York: MDRC.

Millenky, M., D. Bloom, S. Muller-Ravett, and J. Broadus, 2011. *Staying on Course: Three-Year Results of the National Guard Youth ChalleNGe Evaluation.* New York: MDRC.

Miller, Cynthia, Megan Millenky, Lisa Schwartz, Lisbeth Goble, and Jillian Stein, November 2016. *Building a Future: Interim Impact Findings from the YouthBuild Evaluation,* New York: MDRC. As of May 20, 2020:
https://www.mdrc.org/publication/building-future

Moore, K. A., 2006. "Defining the Term 'At-Risk,'" Research to Results brief, Child Trends, Bethesda, Md.

National Center for Education Statistics, undated. "Education Longitudinal Study of 2002 (ELS:2002): User Manuals," webpage, U.S. Department of Education. As of June 12, 2020:
https://nces.ed.gov/surveys/els2002/manuals.asp

———, 2018. "Digest of Education Statistics: 2018," database, U.S. Department of Education. As of May 18, 2020:
https://nces.ed.gov/programs/digest/current_tables.asp

National Center for School Engagement, undated. "Serving At-Risk Youth," webpage. As of May 20, 2020:
http://schoolengagement.org/school-engagement-services/at-risk-youth/

National Guard Youth ChalleNGe, undated. "About the Program," webpage. As of June 11, 2020:
https://ngchallenge.org/about-us/

National Longitudinal Surveys, undated. "National Longitudinal Survey of Youth: Codebook Supplement," webpage, U.S. Bureau of Labor Statistics. As of June 12, 2020:
https://www.nlsinfo.org/content/cohorts/nlsy97/other-documentation/codebook-supplement

———, 1997. *National Longitudinal Survey of Youth: 1997,* Washington, D.C.: U.S. Bureau of Labor Statistics.

NCES—*See* National Center for Education Statistics.

Neild, R. C., and R. Balfanz, 2006. "Unfulfilled Promise: The Dimensions and Characteristics of Philadelphia's Dropout Crisis, 2000–2005," Philadelphia Youth Network, Johns Hopkins University and University of Pennsylvania.

Ou, S.-R., January 2008. "Do GED Recipients Differ from Graduates and School Dropouts?" *Urban Education,* Vol. 43, No. 1, pp. 83–117.

Owens, J., 2004. "A Review of the Social and Non-Market Returns to Education," Education and Learning Wales, Cardiff.

Perez-Arce, F., L. Constant, D. S. Loughran, and L. A. Karoly, 2012. *A Cost-Benefit Analysis of the National Guard Youth ChalleNGe Program*, Santa Monica, Calif.: RAND Corporation, TR-1193-NGYF. As of May 18, 2020: https://www.rand.org/pubs/technical_reports/TR1193.html

Pittman, Robert B., 1991. "Social Factors, Enrollment in Vocational/Technical Courses, and High School Dropout Rates," *Journal of Educational Research*, Vol. 84, No. 5, pp. 288–295.

Pong, S. L., and D. B. Ju, 2000. "The Effects of Change in Family Structures and Income on Dropping Out of Middle and High School," *Journal of Family Issues*, Vol. 21, pp. 147–149.

Ripamonti, E., 2017. "Risk Factors for Dropping Out of High School: A Review of Contemporary, International Empirical Research," *Adolescent Research Review*, Vol. 3, pp. 321–338.

Rivera Drew, Julia A., Sarah Flood, and John Robert Warren, 2014. "Making Full Use of the Longitudinal Design of the Current Population Survey: Methods for Linking Records Across 16 Months," *Journal of Economic and Social Measurement*, Vol. 39, No. 3, pp. 121–144.

Roderick, M., 1994. "Grade Retention and School Dropout: Investigating the Association," *American Education Research Journal*, Vol. 31, pp. 729–759.

Rosenthal, B. S., 1998. "Nonschool Correlates of Dropout: An Integrative Review of the Literature," *Children and Youth Services Review*, Vol. 20, No. 5, pp. 413–433.

Rumberger, R. W., 2004. "Why Students Drop Out of School," in G. Orfield, ed., *Dropouts in America: Confronting the Graduation Rate Crisis*, Cambridge, Mass.: Harvard Education Press.

Schochet, P., J. Burghardt, and S. Glazerman, 2001. *National Job Corps Study: The Impacts of Job Corps on Participants' Employment and Related Outcomes*, Princeton, N.J.: Mathematica Policy Research.

Schochet, P., J. Burghardt, and S. McConnell, 2006. *National Job Corps Study and Longer-Term Follow-up Study: Impact and Benefit-Cost Findings Using Survey and Summary Earnings Records Data*, Princeton, N.J.: Mathematica Policy Research.

———, 2008. "Does Job Corps Work? Impact Findings from the National Job Corps Study," *American Economic Review*, Vol. 98, No. 5, pp. 1864–1886.

Stedman, James B., 1988. *Dropping Out: The Educational Vulnerability of At-Risk Youth*, Washington, D.C.: Congressional Research Service Report for Congress 88 417-EPW.

Suh, S., and J. Suh, 1999. "Risk Factors and Levels of Risk for High School Dropouts," *Professional School Counseling*, Vol. 10, No. 3, pp. 297–306.

Sznitman, S. R., L. Reisel, and A. Khurana, 2017. "Socioeconomic Background and High School Completion: Mediation by Health and Moderation by National Context," *Journal of Adolescence*, Vol. 56, pp. 118–126.

Townsend, L., A. J. Flisher, and G. King, 2007. "A Systematic Review of the Relationship Between High School Dropout and Substance Use," *Clinical Child and Family Psychology*, Vol. 10, No. 7.

Tyler, J. H., 2003. "Economic Benefits of the GED: Lessons from Recent Research," *Review of Educational Research*, Vol. 73, No. 3, pp. 369–403.

———, 2005. "The General Educational Development (GED) Credential: History, Current Research, and Directions for Policy and Practice," in J. Comings, B. Garner, and C. Smith, eds., *Review of Adult Learning and Literacy*, Mahwah, N.J.: Lawrence Erlbaum Associates.

Wang, M. T., and J. A. Fredricks, 2014. "The Reciprocal Links Between School Engagement, Youth Problem Behaviors, and School Dropout During Adolescence," *Child Development*, Vol. 85, pp. 722–737.

Wenger, J. W., L. Constant, W. Chan, K. Edwards, and L. Cottrell, 2019. *National Guard Youth ChalleNGe: Program Progress in 2017–2018*, Santa Monica, Calif.: RAND Corporation, RR-2276-OSD. As of May 19, 2020: https://www.rand.org/pubs/research_reports/RR2276.html

White, S. W., and F. D. Kelly, 2010. "The School Counselor's Role in School Dropout Prevention," *Journal of Counseling and Development*, Vol. 88, pp. 227–235.

Wolfe, B., and R. Haveman, 2002. "Social and Nonmarket Benefits from Education in an Advanced Economy," in Y. K. Kodrzycki, ed., *Education in the 21st Century: Meeting the Challenges of a Changing World*, paper presented at the Federal Reserve Bank of Boston 47th Economic Conference, Boston, Mass., June 19–21.

YouthBuild USA, 2019a. "About YouthBuild USA," webpage. As of May 20, 2020: https://www.youthbuild.org/about-youthbuild-usa

YouthBuild USA, 2019b. "Mission and Philosophy," webpage. As of June 17, 2020: https://www.youthbuild.org/mission-and-philosphy

Youth.Gov, "Reconnecting Youth," undated. Webpage. As of May 20, 2020: https://youth.gov/youth-topics/reconnecting-youth

Zajacova, A., and B. G. Everett, March 2014. "The Nonequivalent Health of High School Equivalents," *Social Science Quarterly*, Vol. 95, No. 1, pp. 221–238.